By William D. Blair, Jr.

Published by The Nature Conservancy

Illustrated by Valerie A. Kells

# KATHARINE ORDWAY

*The Lady Who Saved the Prairies*

*International Standard Book Number: 0–9624590–0–3*
*Library of Congress Catalog Card Number: 89–063300*

*Designed by Robert Wiser and Marc Alain Meadows, Meadows & Wiser,*
*Washington, D.C.*
*Composed in Janson Text (Nicholas Kis) by Meadows & Wiser.*
*Printed on 100# Mohawk Superfine Text by Stephenson, Inc., Alexandria, Virginia.*

*Photography by Susan Bournique, pages 1, 37, 38–39, 51, 55; Wally Dayton, pages 2–3,*
*5; Gary Meszaros, pages 6, 56; Fred Moore, pages 10–11, 69, 115; Bob Unnasch,*
*pages 24–25, 33, 36; Alfred Eisenstaedt, page 29; Clinton White, page 42; Jim Bran-*
*denburg, pages 47, 52, 59; Henry Holdsworth, pages 48, 79; Manhattan Mercury,*
*pages 63, 80; Jack Dykinga, pages 70–71; John Hall, pages 76, 100–101; Alto Adams,*
*page 86; David Boynton, page 89; David Muench, page 90; C. C. Lockwood, page 93;*
*Gary Randorf, page 96; Jeff Lepore, page 109; Steve Schneider, page 112.*

*Page 1: Katharine Ordway's first prairie: the Ordway Prairie Preserve, in western*
*Minnesota.*

*Frontispiece: Umbrella shielding her from the sun, prospective purchaser Ordway*
*inspects the South Dakota grassland which she was to preserve in memory of her cousin,*
*Samuel H. Ordway, Jr.*

*Right: Miss Ordway on the prairie with The Nature Conservancy's Geoffrey Barnard.*

*Page 6: Some of the prairie wildflowers that Katharine Ordway loved.*

*Page 116: Katharine Ordway in later life.*

It was Richard H. Pough who first suggested to me, more than five years ago, that a book of this kind should be published. He felt that Katharine Ordway's extraordinary contribution to the preservation of natural areas in this country — a contribution that had remained essentially anonymous to the day of her death — deserved to be put on the public record.

I thought that was a considerable understatement. The Nature Conservancy, of which I was president at the time of Dick Pough's comment, had been Miss Ordway's principal partner in her conservation work. My colleagues and I were keenly aware of the size of our own and the country's debt to that one individual, whose accomplishment we considered, with some pride for having been involved in it, to be historic. We enthusiastically agreed with Pough's suggestion, and undertook to see to the preparation of a suitable publication, following completion of the preservation programs to which Katharine Ordway's money was still contributing, four years after her death.

In early 1987 I retired from the Conservancy presidency, and with the Ordway programs now winding up, was very pleased to be asked by my successor, Frank D. Boren, to write the appreciation which follows.

I knew that by her own choice, Miss Ordway's exceptional support for land conservation had been largely anonymous while she lived. But when I began my research, I was astonished to discover the extent to which we Americans had managed to ignore one of our important philanthropic benefactors. In the Library of Congress, for example, not a single reference to her was to be found in the periodicals file or the standard biographical references. And the only reference in the book index file was to the catalogue of her art collection, exhibited at Yale. Not a word about conservation — for perhaps the most significant individual donor to that cause of the last half-century, and probably one of the two greatest in our history.

The principal sources of the information presented here are the files of

The Nature Conservancy, including *The Nature Conservancy News;* the minutes and related records of the Goodhill Foundation, which Miss Ordway founded; and the recollections of some of those who knew and worked with her, and with whom I was able to talk. These last have included notably the three long-time confidants and counselors to whom Kay Ordway entrusted her foundation, and most of her fortune, for management after her death: Pough himself, her conservation advisor and friend; John G. Ordway, Jr., her nephew and respected business counselor; and Raymond A. Carter, her lawyer and devoted aide. They also have included John E. Andrus III, Geoffrey S. Barnard, B. Jackson and Lenore Darneille, Wallace C. Dayton, Clifford E. Emanuelson, Richard H. Goodwin, Barbara Barnes Hale, Kiku Hoagland Hanes, Robert E. Jenkins, Riesley R. Jones, Frederick J. and Ann Moore, Patrick F. Noonan, Thomas W. Richards, Bogert F. Thompson, and Joan Ordway Tweedy.

In addition, my own recollections, particularly of the period after I became Conservancy president in April 1980, have doubtless colored this report.

I am indebted also to Arthur H. Brown, Jr., and the New York law firm of Parker and Duryee, and to current members of The Nature Conservancy staff too numerous to thank here individually, for their generous assistance in locating and making available pertinent records.

And I want to thank Joan Tweedy and Raymond Carter for searching out and lending us for publication here some early photographs of Katharine Ordway.

This modest book is not a biography. A full, rounded portrait of an entire life is beyond the scope of this project, though I would be happy if this should help to inspire one. What is attempted here is more limited: a biographical essay on Katharine Ordway's exceptional, and little known, part in the history of environmental protection in this country, and dealing primarily, therefore, with the last quarter of her life. Its sole purpose is to dispel, at least a little, the cloud of secrecy that continues to deny recognition to the lady who saved the prairies.

*W.D.B., Jr.*

# Preparation

*Above: Harebells (bluebells)*

*Overleaf: The Ordway home at Weston, Connecticut.*

*WHEN KATHARINE ORDWAY* died in 1979, the *New York Times* wasted few words in summarizing her achievement:

*A lifetime ecologist and land conservationist, her leadership and contributions to The Nature Conservancy, a national conservation organization, made possible the creation and helped provide for the future maintenance of The Devil's Den–Lucius Pond Ordway Preserve, an open-space, 1,500-acre, wooded wildlife sanctuary in Fairfield County, Connecticut.*

*Her concern for the protection of the nation's natural heritage provided for the establishment in 1971 of the first sanctuary in the Ordway Prairie Preserve System. At the time of her death, the Preserve System, which shelters a wide variety of wildlife and grassland plants, comprised more than 31,000 acres in five midwestern states. The Ordway System is the largest private prairie sanctuary in the world.*

Not mentioned was her legacy to the Goodhill Foundation, which was to multiply her already significant impact on the American natural environment several times over. It was also to put her at the top of the all-time list of private donors to natural-area conservation in this country, rivaled only by the much wealthier John D. Rockefeller, Jr.

Not mentioned also was a striking fact about the life just ended: virtually all of its important work, from a national perspective, at least, had been accomplished in the last 13 of its 80 years.

Three explanations for that fact have been suggested, probably all of them with some justice. In her youth, according to one relative, Kay Ordway was something of a timid soul, inconspicuous in the shadow of her four brothers. A late bloomer, she came only in mid-life to the full self-confidence and sureness of purpose that were to make her a source of strength in her family and beyond.

Raymond Carter, her long-time lawyer and man of affairs, had a simpler explanation. Earlier, he believed, she didn't have the money to be the major philanthropist she became.

A third hypothesis suggests that her interests might have been more productive earlier if she had found the right vehicle for expressing them. But it was not until she had met and heard conservationist Richard Pough, in her 50s, and had come to know The Nature Conservancy, in her 60s, that Katharine Ordway found the way to satisfy her drive to do something about the ecological facts, about environmental decay; something to better, however slightly, the human condition. Once she had found it, she pursued it with a total enthusiasm and vigor that neither age, illness, nor serious injury could dim. And that way was to preserve the land.

Katharine was born on April 3, 1899, to Lucius Pond and Jessie Gilman Ordway, the fourth of five children and the only girl. Her father, then 37, was well on his way to becoming a leading citizen of St. Paul, Minnesota. Born in Brooklyn, New York, and raised in Providence, Rhode Island, he had graduated from Brown University and gone to work in St. Paul for a plumbing and heating supply company. A partner in three years, he had bought out his partner six years later and joined the Crane Company of Chicago in founding Crane and Ordway, later the Crane Company of Minnesota, of which he was to become president and chairman. By 1905 he had earned his first million, or close to it, in plumbing supply and in real estate investments, and was ready to listen when a friend approached him about another investment opportunity.

The opportunity was a struggling young company that had been founded in 1902 to mine corundum, a natural abrasive used to make sandpaper, on the shore of Lake Superior near Two Harbors. Two years later, having sold just $20 worth of the mined mineral (the first sale was the last), the enterprise was on the edge of bankruptcy. But Ordway's friend, Edgar B. Ober, persuaded him that the company could be a success. Ober would supply new day-to-day management; Ordway would provide new capital and oversight.

A deal was made. Ordway and Ober acquired 60 percent of the company's stock; Ober became president. A year later, Ordway had put in $200,000 and wanted out, but couldn't find a buyer for his stock. The company then gave up on its "corundum" — whatever the mineral was, it apparently was not that, and was worthless commercially — and turned creatively to other abrasives. It

*Opposite: Kay Ordway as a child, in St. Paul.*

introduced an abrasive cloth; then the first waterproof sandpaper; then a new kind of industrial masking tape, from which more than 100 other tapes were to evolve, including Scotch Brand cellophane tape. It moved into roofing granules and adhesives. By the time Lucius Ordway died in 1948, sales from Minnesota Mining and Manufacturing Company, later known as "3M," had passed $100 million and were continuing to rise dramatically. By Ray Carter's estimate, the trust fund established for Ordway's five children may have been worth $350 million at his death.

So Katharine Ordway was destined to become a very wealthy woman by her middle age. If she was aware of that fact in her youth, it wasn't early. One of the few recollections of childhood she seems to have passed to others was of overhearing her parents talking, and thinking they must not have any money.

Katharine had a studious bent, which she exercised nearly all her life. She graduated from the University of Minnesota cum laude, with courses in botany and art, foreshadowing what were to become her foremost interests. Later she nearly completed medical school at Yale before deciding against a medical career; she also studied psychology in Europe.

She developed a life-long taste for travel and music, and for clothes, which she would revisit Europe each spring in part to acquire. She became interested in population problems, and visited India with a study group. But while that interest always remained, it was never translated into active participation or support for population work. Pending evidence to the contrary, she had concluded that population limitation was a job for governments, and that the private sector had not shown itself capable of contributing very much to it.

She also traveled all over Europe to study art. She worked at producing art as well, though she was shy about her efforts and kept them from view; her friend Barbara Barnes Hale did see some of her drawings, all of plants.

*Opposite: Young Katharine with her parents, Jessie Gilman and Lucius Pond Ordway; her older brothers John, Samuel, and Lucius Jr. (left to right, rear), and younger brother Richard.*

Katharine had begun collecting, as a young girl, mostly American and European modern art, despite occasional brotherly gibes at her taste and alleged extravagance. She had the last laugh on that. Although she bought what she liked, not what some counselor recommended, she proved to have a perceptive eye for talent. Alan Shestack, then director of the Yale University Art Gallery, was to write of her after her death:

*Katharine Ordway was a remarkable person. Her unassuming, even shy manner gave little evidence of her passion for the causes she espoused and supported, especially the preservation of beauty, both natural and man-made . . . . She created beautiful gardens on her own property . . . . Each acquisition was a personal choice, a commitment based on her own reaction to the character and quality of the object; her decisions never depended on the opinion of curators or critics or on the relative fame of the artist.*

*She saw Brancusi's* Mlle. Pogany *while it was still in the studio and bought it directly from the artist in 1925 . . . . Her Pollack painting was bought . . . in 1948, the year it was painted, long before Pollack became a household name. More often than not, Miss Ordway's intuitions were borne out by subsequent critical judgment.*

Her art collecting was indeed a passion. Barbara Hale recalls her buying "three Mark Rothko's in two or three weeks." Ray Carter never knew her to *sell* a painting. John Andrus, chairman of the Minneapolis Institute of Fine Arts as well as of The Nature Conservancy, was startled at the end of a tour of the art treasures on her New York apartment walls to find a Georges Rouault canvas among the umbrellas and galoshes in her hall closet. She hadn't found room to hang it.

By her later years, her collection was well known to museum directors and sought after. When Shestack first asked if he could see it, she agreed on two conditions: he must not ask for money, and he must not ask for the art. And she had her lawyer with her when Shestack arrived.

After that visit, Shestack was allowed to come again, but on the same two conditions. He never had an inkling until after her death that the gallery he

*Opposite: Plant life and flowers were important from Katharine's girlhood.*

headed was to have the prize. Then he was notified that she had left the collection to Yale University, where her brothers had gone to college and she to medical school, with $2 million for its care and for further acquisitions. She also left $300,000 to establish an exhibit, for which the university museum created a new "Katharine Ordway Gallery" on its second floor.

"The works of art she bought to enhance her own life will now be admired and studied by countless generations of students and will also be available for the public's enjoyment, as Miss Ordway wished," wrote Shestack.

Her art collection was the visible achievement of her earlier life, but it remained the secondary theme. Her interest in conservation had equally strong and deep roots. These included her early courses in botany at the University of Minnesota, which were followed much later, in her 50s, by graduate studies in biology and land-use planning at Columbia University in New York. (At one time in this later period she had a second apartment at 40 Central Park South in New York at least in part to house a laboratory for studying mold.)

Another such root was her love of natural as well as man-made beauty, as Shestack noted. This showed itself among other ways in the places she chose to spend her time — the wooded hills of Connecticut, her principal home; the marshes and dunes of Long Island, New York, with the ocean beyond; the edge of the desert in Arizona, where she often wintered — and in the gardens she created at her homes. Just as she loved her paintings and rarely if ever parted with them, she loved her trees and hated to see any of them cut down. Neighbors in Bridgehampton, her Long Island summer home, once asked her to remove or let them remove some unplanned willow trees that were growing up to block not only their view toward the sea but her own. But the willows were hers, planned or not, and she wouldn't do away with them.

A close friend who encouraged her environmental interests in later years was Barbara Barnes Hale, whose husband, Robert Hale, had been curator of American art at the Metropolitan Museum of New York. As a widow, Barbara Hale lived only a few miles from Bridgehampton, saw much of Katharine Ordway, and traveled with her. She was also a committed and highly active conservationist, and a volunteer naturalist who had helped to introduce many to the

*Kay as a young woman, with her brothers, during World War I.*

fundamentals of our human dependence on nature.

But perhaps the primary influence on Kay Ordway's middle years was a cousin, Samuel Hanson Ordway, Jr. The son of her father's older brother Samuel H. (Sr.), a New York lawyer and judge, Sam Junior was born the year after Katharine, and was a lawyer in New York himself. He was also a co-founder (in 1947– 48) and later head of the Conservation Foundation, one of the first organizations to concern itself with the importance for human welfare of the natural environment as a whole. And he was the author of *Resources for the American Dream* (1953) and other books warning of the impact of population and technology on critical natural resources, including the land.

Katharine Ordway spoke of her cousin Sam often and named a major nature preserve after him, the only member of her family so honored except for her father. And the Conservation Foundation was among the first beneficiaries of small grants from her own foundation, set up in her 60th year (1959) by Ray Carter. She called it the Goodhill Foundation, after the road to her house in Weston, Connecticut, because she didn't want to use her own name. Sam Ordway was one of the first directors of the Goodhill Foundation, whose first grant ($5,000) was to the New York Botanical Gardens.

Presiding as president at the new foundation's first board of directors meeting, in June 1959, Katharine Ordway announced that her primary charitable interests were "population control, conservation, art, and scholarships for research in pure science," and requested that these interests be honored in the event of her death. But by 1962, she had advised the directors that her "primary charitable interest is the preservation of open land," with "the emphasis [to] be on keeping the land wild and not developing [it] for the amusement or entertainment of people." From then on, land conservation was her major goal.

In some ways, this was surprising. The stereotypical wilderness enthusiast is a rugged outdoors person — a hiker, canoeist, hunter, angler, or the like. While young Katharine had shared in her family's sailing activity as a child — her father had been a founder and first commodore of the White Bear Yacht Club and winner of its first regatta — she was far from rugged physically, and cautious to the point of being "afraid of a germ," in a relative's words. She moved east at least in part because she felt the cold keenly and didn't like the long Minnesota winter or its storms. Small and thin, she had also become somewhat hunchbacked, which affected her walk and required special attention to her clothes by her seamstress, Ann Moore, wife of her caretaker, gardener, and chauffeur at Weston, Frederick Moore. Having sensitive skin, she habitually carried an umbrella to shade her from strong sunlight. In later life she suffered from osteoporosis and repeated injuries, like a broken hip when a pet springer spaniel knocked her down (it was her only pet, and she felt it best to give him away), and two wrists broken simultaneously on another occasion. Increasingly frail, she reminded more than one acquaintance of a bird — "a little wren," Patrick Noonan found her; "delicate, but with piercing eyes and inner strength." "Like a bird fallen out of the nest," to Barbara Hale, "but great stamina. She was tough, tough, tough!"

As these descriptions suggest, she gained greatly in confidence over the years; the girl who was afraid of a germ wound up traveling to even the most unhygienic areas of the world, and afraid of nothing. Frederick Moore recalls her shaking her fist at a motorist who displeased her; when the motorist then followed them to Katharine's garage to express his own anger, she was undaunted. By then she knew what she wanted and wasn't afraid to ask for it. It showed in small ways: "She would give me an hour and ten minutes to get to New York from Weston," Moore remembers, "and if I didn't make it, she wanted to know why." And it showed in her philanthropy.

By the 1960s, if not earlier — in her 60s herself — Katharine Ordway had the interest, the confidence, and the money to make a major contribution to conservation. All that was lacking was the right person, and the right project, to provide the spark.

# Devil's Den

*Above: Red trillium with lightning bug*

*Overleaf: The first preserve: Lucius Pond Ordway Preserve–Devil's Den, in Fairfield County, southwestern Connecticut*

IN THE 1950s, numerous members of New York–area garden clubs were among the participants in a monthly Conservation Round Table at the American Museum of Natural History. Katharine Ordway attended on occasion and became acquainted with Richard H. Pough, the moving spirit of the Round Table and the chairman of the museum's Conservation and General Ecology Department.

In 1956 Pough left the museum and founded the Natural Areas Council, to muster support for conservation causes full-time. His prime concern was the disappearance of natural areas, in particular in and around the East Coast megalopolis. He began to appeal to the larger landowners of his acquaintance, urging them to work with conservation organizations to preserve their open land, and his efforts met with some success.

This appealed to Katharine Ordway, who loved her own land and was one day to preserve it. As Pough recalls, she approached him with a challenge: "You're just doing this hit or miss. If I give you some seed money, will you organize to do it systematically?"

Pough was delighted. Enlisting the help of Sam Ordway, writer-conservationist William H. Whyte, and former Nature Conservancy President James B. Ross, he set up an Open Space Committee (later the Open Space Institute) to publicize the need for open space and solicit land for it. The Ordway seed money came in the form of a $30,000 grant to the committee in 1964 from the Goodhill Foundation, through the Conservation Foundation. Sam Ordway commented to the other Goodhill directors that there was "too little park and recreation space" in suburban areas and that "land for public use in those areas, in the East particularly, is rapidly disappearing."

Pough then hired an advertising-agency copywriter and produced a brochure to send to every large private landowner within 100 miles of New York, telling them how other private landowners had preserved their land. He also hired field men to search for important and unprotected open space and to follow up with any landowner who showed signs of interest. "Go and look the property over a bit first," he told them, "and find something — a pond, a row of beech trees, anything to be ecstatic about when you see the owners. Then talk about the future of their land."

Katharine Ordway joined in meetings of the Open Space Committee and was enthusiastic. She pledged that if the committee turned up an undeveloped area worthy of permanent preservation and no other solution offered, she would buy it.

One of those who heard this pledge was Clifford E. Emanuelson, the field representative assigned to Fairfield County, Connecticut. Exploring the county, he found a 1,200-acre tract of beautiful forest that the Bridgeport Hydraulic Company wanted to sell but also wanted to remain undeveloped, to protect the watershed. In that time and place, so close to New York City, 1,200 wild and unprotected acres were already a rare find. And Katharine Ordway lived only a few minutes' drive away. The opportunity was plain; all that was needed was someone to take responsibility for caring for the land once it was purchased.

Emanuelson approached the local public authorities; no interest there. Talks with local conservationists followed. Finally, he and Dick Pough, then a Conservancy board member, approached The Nature Conservancy through its Connecticut Chapter and national president, Richard H. Goodwin, a botanist at Connecticut College, and another nearby board member and former president, Alexander B. Adams. The Conservancy was eager to have the property as a preserve. And so a marriage was made between Katharine Ordway and the Conservancy that was to affect the course of natural-area preservation in this country significantly for the next 20 years.

The principal marriage broker was an extraordinary figure. Born in Brooklyn in 1904 and trained at the Sloan School of Management at the Massachusetts Institute of Technology, Richard Pough had started his career in

*Opposite: Richard H. Pough, "America's conservation matchmaker" and a long-time friend and advisor to Katharine Ordway, founded the Open Space Committee (later Institute) with her help. Also a founder and early president of The Nature Conservancy, he helped to bring that organization and Miss Ordway together in a partnership which was to last for 14 years until her death in 1979, and through the foundation which she established, even beyond.*

*Fifteen miles of foot trails and at least a score of 19th-century charcoal-burning sites mark the woodlands of the "Devil's Den" preserve (above), an extraordinary wilderness remnant to have survived only an hour's drive from New York City. Here a demonstration of charcoal making is being prepared.*

engineering jobs in Texas and Missouri, then bought a retail business in Philadelphia. But his heart wasn't in it; what he really liked to do was watch birds. In 1936, at the age of 32, he turned his business over to a brother and joined the National Audubon Society staff in New York. Twelve years later he moved to the American Museum of Natural History as its senior ecologist and conservation activist. In these years he also wrote three widely known volumes of Audubon Bird Guides.

After nearly a decade, in 1956–57, Pough left the museum, where he had been, if anything, a little too much of an activist for some of his colleagues and directors, and founded his Natural Areas Council. His dedication to his vocation was now total. From this point until his retirement in 1984, at age 80, he occupied a unique and self-made position in the environmental movement as what one writer called "America's conservation matchmaker." Pough earned this title by helping to found, counseling, and often heading as a volunteer a long list of local, regional, and national conservation organizations, and above all helping to fund them, by discovering, motivating, and soliciting potential major donors and introducing them to organizations ready to apply their major gifts to protecting the environment. In addition to the Open Space Institute and the Audubon Society, he played a prominent role at various times in such organizations as the World Wildlife Fund, America the Beautiful Fund, Association for the Protection of the Adirondacks, Defenders of Wildlife, and The Nature Conservancy, among many, many others.

Of none of his involvements was Pough more proud than of the launching of The Nature Conservancy, which he co-founded in 1950 and headed as president from 1952 to 1956. His primary concern was always the land. "My basic interest over the past 40 years," he wrote to a correspondent in 1982, "has been in seeing whether steps could be taken before it is too late to insure that coming generations have at least a few undisturbed examples of each of the distinctive plant and animal communities (often called ecotypes) of the United States." And The Nature Conservancy was committed to preserving the most important remaining natural land, the sole national organization exclusively dedicated to that task.

The Conservancy's origins traced back to the Ecological Society of America, founded in 1915 by a group of scientists sparked by Victor Shelford, an assistant professor of zoology at the University of Illinois. In 1926 the Society published "The Naturalist's Guide to the Americas," which warned of the disappearance of natural areas, and began lobbying for their preservation. After World War II the Society decided to stick to scientific study and renounce preservation action, and Shelford and other activist leaders, including Dick Pough, resigned to found the Ecologists' Union. In 1950 the Union changed its name to The Nature Conservancy to attract support from the non-scientist public and began to call for a national system of natural-area preserves.

The new Conservancy was incorporated in Washington, D.C., a year later "to preserve or aid in the preservation of all types of wild nature," and its first significant project was "A Preliminary Inventory of Nature Sanctuaries in the United States and Canada." With natural areas visibly shrinking everywhere, the scientists contributing to this survey were disturbed not to have found a single natural community type in North America north of Mexico that was sufficiently well represented in nature reserves to be considered safe.

In 1954 came the opportunity that was to set the pattern for the Conservancy's future. A local group in Westchester County, New York, was trying to save a deep ravine on the Mianus River, near the Connecticut border, from sale for development. The site featured a waterfall, a virgin hemlock stand, and old-growth hardwood trees. After months of unsuccessful negotiations, the landowner presented an ultimatum: buy now, or else. The group scraped together a down payment and turned to the Conservancy for help.

The Conservancy agreed to try. With Ernest Brooks of the Old Dominion Foundation, also a Conservancy board member, Pough came up with a

*Opposite: Godfrey Pond on the Lucius Pond Ordway Preserve. The 1,500-acre Devil's Den sanctuary includes several brooks and a variety of forest types on the wetlands and slopes, with rocky crests partly covered with grasses, mosses, and lichens. It embraces much of the watershed of the West Branch of the Saugatuck River.*

novel idea for a grant. If the Old Dominion Foundation (founded by Paul Mellon) would put up the rest of the money needed to buy the land, the Conservancy would lend the money to the local Mianus project committee. The committee would then be expected to raise the money to pay it back, with low interest, over a reasonable period. After that, the Conservancy could use the same funds for another project, again to be repaid by local fund raising, and so on, indefinitely. A modest grant would revolve through a number of projects, with results disproportionate to its size. Local enthusiasm could be harnessed across the country, to national effect.

Old Dominion put up the $7,500 still needed, and the ravine was saved, to remain a beautiful and popular Conservancy preserve, which has multiplied in size nearly tenfold since the original 60-acre purchase. The project, and the idea, put the young organization in business. It showed that money could be raised and important natural land acquired, despite development competition. Not for a decade, when Katharine Ordway as an individual and the Ford Foundation as an institution began to make major investments in it, was The Nature Conservancy to take a comparable leap forward.

Such were the partners with whom Kay Ordway undertook to preserve the Devil's Den, in Fairfield County.

The property itself undoubtedly inspired the buyer. Part of the largest wilderness tract left in southwestern Connecticut, it had been popularly named by the early settlers for an outsized "footprint" in a large rock, which "could only have been made by the devil." It was hilly, with rugged rock outcroppings forming cliffs and high ledges. From the crests, on a clear day, a visitor could see Long Island, 25 miles away across the Sound.

By the 1920s, the 19th-century American chestnut forest there had been eliminated by blight, but decaying chestnut logs were still to be seen along the trails, covered with lichens and mosses. Still present today, the Den's forest was then nearly a century old — oak on the upper slopes, beech, birch, and sugar maple on the lower, red maple wetlands below. Five hundred species of vascular plants could be found here, including sweetgum trees, rare at the edge of their range; the fauna included increasingly uncommon timber rattlesnakes and eastern copperheads. Archaeological evidence indicated human use of the area, mostly for hunting, as much as 5,000 years ago; charcoal burning, a big industry in the 1800s, had marked dozens of sites.

As the crow flies, the Devil's Den began just 35 miles from the Bronx.

On January 17, 1966, The Nature Conservancy purchased 463 acres from the water company and two adjacent small landowners. The money came from Katharine Ordway, whose previous association with the organization was a $25 membership in 1962 and a $200 life membership two years later. Now, in her first project contribution, she put up $118,000 through the Goodhill Foundation and $136,000 directly, by gift of 2,000 shares of 3M stock. For Goodhill, it was the first six-figure grant. At the donor's request, the Conservancy agreed in writing that the land was to be "preserved or maintained in its natural state and used solely for conservation of its natural beauty and resources, research . . . and nature study by and through spiritual refreshment . . . ."

In memory of Katharine's father, the sanctuary was called the Lucius Pond Ordway Preserve–Devil's Den, and it grew rapidly under her personal care and the Conservancy's in the years that followed. Within three or four years she had financed the acquisition of nearly 1,400 acres and the hiring of Cliff Emanuelson as preserve director and begun the planning of a manager's house and the establishment of a substantial endowment. This last was a precedent she was infrequently to follow afterward; she preferred her dollars to be used for acquiring the land rather than for managing it thereafter. In all, she and her foundation were to put more than $1.5 million into the Devil's Den.

Today, properties of the towns of Weston and Redding and of the Bridgeport Hydraulic Company adjoin the sanctuary, and the last inholding has been bought out by the Conservancy; so the 1,565-acre Lucius Pond Ordway Preserve is probably within a few acres of its destined full size. The preserve now includes 15 miles of hiking trails in much of the watershed of the West Branch of the Saugatuck River and all of the watershed of four substantial "brooks." Open land in Fairfield County, possibly the richest county in the richest state

in the union, currently sells for $150,000 an acre and more — a price at which the preserve, in other respects priceless, could now be worth a quarter of a billion dollars.

Clearly moved by her satisfying experience with the Devil's Den project, President Ordway circulated a written statement to the other Goodhill Foundation directors at their annual meeting in November 1970 for discussion and approval: "You know that conservation and population control are my principal interests. It is my wish that these interests be continued as the objectives of the Foundation after my death. It is my wish that the major portion of the Foundation's principal and income be used in acquiring land or in furthering the acquisition of land for conservation purposes."

She was now nearly 72 years old, and she had found her calling.

It was not too late.

*Opposite: Rock outcrops at the "Den." Katharine Ordway's success in acquiring and protecting this wild tract as a nature reserve was the springboard for her extraordinary career, late in life, in saving natural land. She was sure to be at Weston in the autumn to see the glorious New England foliage display around her home and the preserve which she had created.*

# The Prairie System

Above: Pasqueflower with honeybee

Overleaf: Katharine Ordway wanted to preserve for future generations the sight
of winds sweeping through the prairie grasses.

By 1969 LAND ACQUISITION for the Devil's Den preserve had been largely completed. For all the parties to it, the success and satisfactions of the project demanded repetition. The question was on what land to focus.

Pough had more than open space in mind. He knew that Kay Ordway remained at heart a native of Minnesota, a prairie state. And he knew that "of all the types of land that needed preservation and were least protected, prairies were at the top." Saving the prairies was a major need, and she could play a major role.

The prairies, natural grasslands, once covered nearly one-fifth of North America — the most extensive of its natural systems. With numerous variations, prairies lay generally in three zones, from the foot of the Rockies to the edge of the hardwood forests of the East. Across the high plains from Montana south to New Mexico and west Texas grew the short, tough buffalo grass, blue grama, western wheat grass, and cacti of the shortgrass prairie. From the Dakotas to Indiana and south to east Texas and Louisiana, with scattered patches farther east, stretched the tallgrass prairie, with big bluestem grass its symbol, and Indian grass and prairie cordgrass, all growing up to eight or ten feet tall in summer in a good year and waving in a breeze like the ocean swell. In between was a shifting zone of mid-grasses, expanding and contracting with changing conditions, with a mixture of species from both.

Water and soil made the difference. The tallgrass prairie evolved under greater annual rainfall than fell in the shadow of the mountains farther west, and on more productive soils.

Occasional drought encouraged lightning-ignited fires. The droughts, the fires, and the great herds of grazing animals — bison especially, and elk, deer, and in some areas pronghorn, which ate the tender emerging stalks of woody vegetation and killed it but kept moving and didn't permanently damage the other plant cover — prevented the forest from replacing the grasses and wildflowers.

The prairie, in particular the tallgrass prairie, was a bountiful estate. Some 80 species of mammals lived in the tallgrass. Hares, rabbits, and voles

*The bison, a prominent part of the original prairie ecosystem, was all but wiped out a century ago. Today the "buffalo" roams again on four major grassland preserves which Katharine Ordway and her foundation helped to create, in Kansas (Konza Prairie), South Dakota (Samuel H. Ordway, Jr., Memorial Prairie), North Dakota (Cross Ranch), and Nebraska (Niobrara Prairie).*

devoured the grass; ground squirrels and harvest mice ate the seed; pocket gophers consumed the underground tubers and roots. Wolves, coyotes, foxes, weasels, shrews, hawks, owls, and snakes preyed on the vegetarians. Birds and plants of the prairie, many of the latter wildflowers, ran to the hundreds of species.

The tightly woven roots and tough underground stems (rhizomes) of the tallgrass prairie made the soil so dense that it couldn't be tilled without a special sod-breaking plow. But the deep topsoil was rich in humus and nutrients, a potential gold mine for farmers. Once a suitable plow had been developed in the 19th century, the tallgrass rapidly disappeared.

Today, the former tallgrass prairie region is the Corn Belt, the breadbasket of the United States and half the world. Once an estimated 400,000 square miles in extent, or more than a quarter-billion acres, the tallgrass survives only in scattered fragments, as in early settlers' graveyards or along old fenced railroad rights of way. In Iowa the largest tract left is reportedly 200 acres. In Illinois, "the Prairie State," once at least half tallgrass, nearly all the unploughed prairie parcels of more than one acre on the characteristic deep black loam soil are gone.

Although the short- and mixed-grass prairies have been shrinking at a lesser rate, agricultural and other development, and notably overgrazing by domestic livestock, have been degrading and destroying them progressively as well.

Tallgrass has been little protected in public preserve systems. In the early 1930s efforts to establish a state Tallgrass Prairie Preserve in Illinois drew strong support from the Illinois legislature, the National Research Council, and the Ecological Society of America — until it was discovered that the last suitable prairie in the state had been plowed up.

In 1962 bills were introduced in Congress to create a Tallgrass Prairie National Park, and a Senate subcommittee held hearings on them in Kansas, the most likely site. The bills died in subcommittee because of opposition from cattlemen in the range states, who wanted no diminution of actual or potential grazing land and argued that grasshoppers would spread like a plague from the park to private lands. Another try in 1971, supported by the governor of Kansas and the federal Department of the Interior, was again opposed by ranchers and failed. Some recent attempts have focused on Oklahoma, but in 1989 they were still some distance from success.

When Dick Pough talked about the prairies back in the late 1960s, Katharine Ordway was a willing listener. She knew and loved the prairie, for its gay profusion of flowers most of all. As a student of botany, she recognized its rich plant life as an important natural resource. And she had vivid childhood memories of her mother talking about the "prairie schooners" heading west from St. Paul and disappearing across the endless seas of grass. Future generations of Americans, she thought, should have the opportunity to learn what that nation-building voyage was like for their pioneer ancestors.

At first it was only the prairie remnants in Minnesota that she wanted to save. She was always loyal to Minnesota and thought the state and its people were special; "something in the water," she said. And it was a good place to start. Native grassland had once covered about a quarter of the state's land, or around 20,000 square miles; now only perhaps 20 square miles, or one-tenth of 1 percent of it, remained in anything close to its original condition, and that was diminishing day by day. "In the past six years," the Minnesota Chapter of The Nature Conservancy was to report in 1972, eight [prairie parcels] that we have wanted have been lost. One is now a cornfield, one is a Christmas tree plantation, one is [now] heavily overgrazed and full of introduced European weeds, one has been scalped for sod . . . two have been mined for gravel, one is an industrial site and one particularly fine one has been purchased by speculators and its price is utterly out of reach."

The Conservancy in fact had acquired a handful of prairie tracts since the late 1950s, several of them in Minnesota, and all of them very small. Pough's report to the staff on Kay Ordway's interest in prairies was eagerly received, especially by Conservancy President Thomas W. Richards; by Patrick F. Noonan, who had just joined in 1969 and quickly became Director of Operations and senior real-estate dealmaker (and was to become president himself, at age 29, in 1973); and by the Midwestern staff headquartered in Minneapolis and its director, Riesley R. Jones.

In May 1970 the Midwest office supplied a list of suggested prairie properties it would like to acquire. Noonan forwarded it to Kay Ordway. In December, with her approval and funds, the Conservancy made the first purchase from the list.

This first prairie was actually a second choice. They had wanted to buy another, larger tract, but the owner wanted to market its gravel and wouldn't sell. Still, this was 310 acres of tallgrass — prize enough, by the Conservancy's current standards. One of the least disturbed grassland tracts left in Minnesota, it had never been plowed, and parts of it were believed never even to have been grazed by cattle or mowed. The profusion of plant life included big bluestem in abundance, and pasqueflower and prairie smoke and a rainbow of other wildflowers. Six miles southwest of the town of Brooten in the western part of the state, it sloped up to a ridgetop with spectacular views of the surrounding hills and valleys.

Gratefully, the Conservancy named it the Katharine Ordway Prairie Preserve. At the time the donor raised no objection, but a few years later she requested that the "Katharine" in the name be dropped and the site known simply as the Ordway Preserve, and the change was made. A very private person, she never again allowed her own name, as distinct from the Ordway family name, to be used to label a preserve. It wasn't until after her death that another sanctuary was named for her.

In quick succession, the Ordway/Conservancy team then acquired three more Minnesota prairie fragments, all in the western part of the state: Wahpeton Prairie (named for a subtribe of the Santee Sioux that had hunted the area), 80 acres of upland above the Cottonwood River in Redwood County; Santee Prairie in Mahnomen County, 448 acres of wet prairie dotted with glacial potholes — prime waterfowl habitat; and Chippewa Prairie, the initial piece, 80 acres of tall- and mixed-grass prairie on an abandoned river terrace along Lac Qui Parle ("the lake that talks") on the Minnesota River, near the South Dakota border.

The last buy was made for a special purpose. The Lac Qui Parle locale was considered the best site available for the reintroduction of the greater prairie chicken in its former range in the state, now greatly reduced. This grassland bird had come close to extinction, along with its habitat. Its eastern race, the mid-Atlantic heath hen, was believed to have been extinct since the 1930s. Its southern race, Attwater's prairie chicken, once a million strong along the Texas and Louisiana coasts, had been eliminated completely in Louisiana and was down to two sites in southeast Texas. Protection of habitat for the dwindling northern subspecies was a high priority for The Nature Conservancy in the Midwest. And only on undisturbed tallgrass prairie would the bird's "booming" call be heard in the dawn, as it strutted and danced and displayed its bright throat sacs to win a mate.

Kay Ordway was to finance several additions to the original Chippewa Prairie and to live to see the prairie chicken returned there. By 1987 the Conservancy had built the preserve to nearly 1,000 acres.

The Indian names for the natural areas were chosen at the donor's request. Clifford Emanuelson recalls making this suggestion to her. Responding to her request, Rick Jones in the Midwest Conservancy office investigated and located the "cultural centers" of the pertinent Indian tribes and stockpiled a list of appropriate names in different areas, for use as needed. And the list was soon exhausted; "when we ran out of names of suitable tribes, we had to use the Indian names for tallgrass, and prairie chicken, and running water, and so on," according to Jones's successor, Geoffrey S. Barnard.

Despite her initial preference for Minnesota sites, Katharine Ordway had recognized almost immediately the arguments for ranging farther afield. Good surviving prairie was hard to find, and when found needed protection in *all* of the states of its former presence. The Conservancy list of target prairie properties had included some non-Minnesota choices from the beginning.

*The greater prairie chicken. In 1971, the prairie surrounding Lac Qui Parle on the Minnesota River was considered the best site available for reintroduction of this endangered bird to a part of its former range in Minnesota. A tract in this area was one of Miss Ordway's first prairie purchases, and she lived to see the endangered bird returned there.*

*Black ducks on Lac Qui Parle ("The Lake That Talks"). A 2,000-acre Central Flyway waterfowl refuge has been established on this prairie wetland by The Nature Conservancy, the state, and the U.S. Fish and Wildlife Service. Katharine Ordway helped to fund the land acquisition, personally and later through her Goodhill Foundation.*

What was needed was a planned preserve *system*, to include the best — least altered — remaining examples of all the different variations of tallgrass prairie, wherever located.

So in 1971, while funding acquisition of the three Minnesota grasslands, Katharine Ordway also approved and funded three purchases in other states: Pawnee Prairie, in southeastern Nebraska near the Kansas border, a 320-acre parcel next to a state park, with a remnant population of greater prairie chickens; Sioux Prairie, in South Dakota, 35 miles north of Sioux Falls, 80 acres of rolling tallgrass with buffalo rubbing rocks and wallows still evident, and good enough to have been used for research by the state university (an additional 80 acres was bought the following year); and Konza Prairie, in the Flint Hills of Kansas. This was to become perhaps her greatest achievement, although that wasn't clear at the start.

The Nature Conservancy in 1971 was used to small preserves. As a relatively new and unendowed organization in a capital-intensive and highly expensive field, land, it had had to be. Katharine Ordway didn't really like small preserves. She could enjoy the beauty of them, and she could understand their importance when they represented a last chance. But what she wanted to preserve more than anything else was the experience of those vast expanses of grass.

"We had a hard time finding big, high-quality parcels, even after we got over our hump of thinking small," Noonan remembers. "And she'd say, 'Can't you get me a prairie that we can go out on and not see *anything* else — no houses, no power lines, *anything*?' So we went and got Konza."

It wasn't by any means as simple as that.

Scores of articles, popular and technical, have been written about Konza, and at least one enthusiastic book (*Konza Prairie, A Tallgrass Natural History*, by O. J. Reichman, University Press of Kansas, 1987). Understandably, they tend not to dwell on the time and effort it took to make Konza the major prairie reserve that it is today.

Since the late 1950s, a group of faculty members from five departments of Kansas State University had been searching the northern Flint Hills of Kansas for the best remaining prairie. Headed by biologist Lloyd C. Hulbert, the team wanted the scarce native grassland for protection and use as the site of a research center for the study of tallgrass prairie — its origins, ecology, and abundant productivity.

The Flint Hills, running north and south across eastern Kansas from the Nebraska border into Oklahoma, lie at the western edge of the original tallgrass prairie. Large areas of the prairie here are steep and rocky and unsuitable for cultivation, and hence have been saved. This is almost the only place left where good natural tallgrass stretching for thousands of acres can be found. Even in the Flint Hills, deep soils without rocks are scarce, and only a small part of Konza today has unplowed deep soil. That part adds significantly to Konza's value for research.

Hulbert's search was prolonged, partly by the difficulty of finding some deep uncultivated soil, partly by the lack of purchase money. He approached various federal agencies; they couldn't help. In the mid-1960s he approached The Nature Conservancy, which was interested and promptly opened negotiations for the land at the top of Hulbert's list. It was too late; the property had been sold for other uses before a Conservancy offer was made.

Hulbert's second choice included a tract of fine tallgrass a few miles south of Kansas State University at Manhattan, owned by Theo Cobb Landon, second wife of former governor and Republican presidential candidate Alfred M. Landon. In early 1971, with Katharine Ordway's potential support in mind, the Conservancy and the university discussed a possible approach to the Landons.

Almost immediately, the Conservancy heard a polite protest from the governor's office in Topeka. The governor, Robert B. Docking, had set up a special

*Opposite: Milkweed seed pods on the prairie in the Flint Hills of Kansas, at the western edge of the original tallgrass zone. This was almost the only area left where largely unaltered natural tallgrass prairie extending for thousands of acres could still be found. For Katharine Ordway, The Nature Conservancy and Kansas State University searched here, and found Konza.*

*The Flint Hills. Miss Ordway established two tallgrass preserves there: one in southern Kansas, of 2,200 acres; the other, 70 miles to the north, nearly 9,000 acres, the largest protected tallgrass prairie in the country. This was to become the Konza Prairie Research Natural Area and to be recognized by UNESCO as an International Biosphere Reserve.*

commission to promote a Prairie National Park in Kansas and was afraid that the Conservancy project might undermine his own. He registered his concern by sending the head of his commission to Washington, to appeal to Conservancy decision-makers. The latter agreed to hold off for three to six months. But as they had expected, the governor's Prairie National Park effort went no further than earlier attempts. In June Noonan flew to Kansas to ask the Landons to consider donating the land for preservation.

The Landons weren't interested in a gift, but they were willing to consider a swap of 916 acres for a slightly larger piece nearby. Noonan wanted more, but negotiations for another 600 acres were unsuccessful. In the fall the swap land was acquired, with Ordway funds, and the trade was completed on the next-to-last day of the year. The Conservancy transferred title to the tract to the university, for preservation and the establishment of a prairie research center.

It wasn't yet the really big tallgrass prairie that Katharine Ordway, the Conservancy, and the university all wanted. It had problems, as a preserve and as a research center. Several of its watersheds began on the ranch next door and therefore couldn't be controlled. In addition, reproducing and studying the native tallgrass prairie system required both grazing by native grazers — bison, elk, pronghorn — and, from time to time, burning, as the natural grassland had burned. But the scientists agreed that the 900 acres were not enough to support reintroduction of the wild grazing herds. They would study fire impacts first and continue to seek more land.

Nevertheless, it was a start, and the biggest unit yet in the growing Ordway Prairie Preserve System.

At first, Katharine Ordway was resistant. She didn't like the idea of state ownership or control, even through a university. But in the end, the potential size and importance of the prairie, and the combined persuasion of Pough, Richards, Noonan, and others, won her over.

She wanted this preserve, too, to bear an Indian name. It was decided to name it after the tribe for which the state was named, whose villages had been scattered along the Kansas River until the occupants were forced west in the 1800s. There were many spellings of the tribal name, such as "Kaw," an abbreviation, and "Kansa," now the more or less accepted version. The university proposed using the "o" spelling ("Konza") to avoid the appearance of a misspelling of Kansas, and that was adopted.

At the end of 1971, most of the ultimate Konza Preserve was still to be protected. But it had been quite a year. The following spring, *The Nature Conservancy News* reviewed the year's accomplishments and reported: "Of special significance in 1971 is the creation of the Ordway Prairie Preserve System, which during the year added nearly 2,000 acres of virgin prairie and six new sanctuaries to the Conservancy's list of grassland habitats saved." In a rare departure from her anonymity rule, the magazine told Conservancy members that the "funds to purchase these acres [had been] generously made available by Miss Katharine Ordway." As a result of these and earlier efforts, The Nature Conservancy had now "stepped to the fore as the primary prairie preserve group in the nation."

It was only the beginning. Thereafter, acquisition continued rapidly.

That year, 1972, Miss Ordway whetted her appetite by making at least two trips to visit her preserves and potential preserves — one to her Chippewa Prairie in Minnesota, one to a new Osage Prairie Preserve site, among others she funded in Missouri that year. Pough and the Conservancy had been recommending Missouri to her. According to the Missouri Prairie Foundation, at least one-third of the state, or 15 million acres, had once been tallgrass prairie. Less than 1 percent of that remained, including only three tracts as big as a section (640 acres) in the whole state. Osage Prairie was the largest single unit of virgin prairie known in Missouri: 1,115 acres of rolling hills in Vernon

*Opposite: Big bluestem grass on Osage Prairie, Missouri. Among hundreds of prairie plants, big bluestem is the hallmark of the tallgrass prairie, along with Indian grass; both can grow to more than eight feet. Little bluestem and such showy prairie flowers as coneflower, leadplant, catclaw, and prairie clover are also conspicuous here.*

County in the southwestern part of the state, with an active prairie chicken booming ground, and even more rare, a prairie stream with river birch shading its banks. Kay Ordway agreed to fund its purchase, and an 80-acre addition to it three years later, when it became available, to protect a continuous mile and a half of the stream.

She was less happy about The Nature Conservancy's "Project '76," to protect several thousand additional acres of Missouri's remaining prairie in small fragments. This was to be done in cooperation with the Missouri Prairie Foundation and the state's Department of Conservation over the four years to 1976, as a Bicentennial gift to the nation. But she recognized that there was no acceptable alternative ("it is no longer realistic to consider only those areas of 1,000 acres or more," wrote the Prairie Foundation's wildlife biologist, Donald M. Christisen), and she went along. As a result, a dozen small new preserves, initially of 40 to 320 acres (some were added to later), were established in rapid succession, all in southwestern Missouri, all with Indian names like Pawhuska and Wah'Kon-Tah.

The Missouri effort, which brought the principal donor a letter of warm thanks from Governor Christopher S. Bond on behalf of the people of his state, was capped in 1978–79, after the Bicentennial, by the acquisition of land for a 2,000-acre Missouri Prairie State Park.

At the same time, in the mid-1970s, Katharine Ordway was adding small tracts to her preserve system in Minnesota. She was also establishing a second substantial preserve, of 2,200 acres, in the Flint Hills 75 miles south of Konza, in part as a possible nucleus for a future Tallgrass Prairie National Park, still under discussion for this area in southeastern Kansas. And in the back of her

*Opposite: Prairie-dock (here on Pawhuska Prairie, Missouri) grows up to ten feet tall and blooms in yellow profusion in late summer and early fall. Before settlers came, tallgrass prairie covered at least 15 million acres of what is now Missouri. By the 1970s, no more than half of 1 percent of this remained. The same trend was clear in the other prairie states.*

mind, she was looking for an outstanding sanctuary to dedicate to the memory of her cousin Sam, who had died in 1971.

In early 1975 the Conservancy thought it had found one for her — not tallgrass, primarily, but 7,500 acres of mixed-grass prairie in fine condition, with 400 wetlands, from tiny potholes to good-sized glacial lakes, in addition. Located 30 miles northwest of Aberdeen, in north-central South Dakota, the wetlands were part of the most productive waterfowl habitat in North America — the pothole country of the Dakotas, western Minnesota, and central Canada — and hosted 2,000 pairs of nesting ducks in a wet year: blue-winged teal, mallards, pintails, shovelers, canvasbacks, and ruddy ducks among others, along with small flocks of white pelicans.

In the wet bottoms, lush clumps of big bluestem, slough grass, and canary grass thrived. Along the drier hillsides, little bluestem, june grass, and needlegrass took their place. On the hilltops, retaining the least moisture, blue grama and buffalo grass provided lower cover. The ground was rough and stony, which had protected it from plowing, and the plant cover had been protected by the good ranching practices of a long-time owner, who had rotated his cattle among different pastures and rested pastures altogether from time to time to keep grazing light. Pronghorn antelopes had been reintroduced in the area several years earlier and now were frequenting the ranch.

The property was in demand for research and field studies by various colleges and schools, and the current owner was willing to sell at less than fair market value. It was almost too good to be true, and the Conservancy was nervous. For one thing, this would be its biggest purchase yet. For another, this wasn't a tallgrass prairie, exactly, and how would Katharine Ordway react to it? Noonan and Barnard had flown to Charleston, South Carolina, where she was visiting, to tell her about it, and she had agreed in principle to buy it, but she wanted to see it first. And The Nature Conservancy was already committed; it had had to make a decision before she got there — exercise its option to buy, or risk losing the property — and had chosen the former. With the purchase price near $1.5 million, the effect would be serious if she changed her mind.

*Above: Jim Brandenburg's photo of a ferruginous hawk with chicks at their nest in the needlegrass on the Samuel Ordway Memorial Prairie. Kay Ordway dedicated the reserve to her conservationist cousin, co-founder of the Conservation Foundation and author of* Resources for the American Dream *and other books sounding early environmental warnings.*

The Conservancy mobilized a strong team to show her the proposed reserve: Wallace C. Dayton, member of a distinguished Minneapolis family, long-time Conservancy volunteer leader and former chairman, and a major donor himself; G. Jon Roush, executive vice president of the organization and Montana ranch-owner; and Geoff Barnard, vice president and Midwestern regional director. They gathered in Minneapolis in June, and there was a certain tension in the air, of which the central figure was well aware. Mischievously, she joked, "I'm sure this is going to be a fine tallgrass prairie, with lots of flowers."

Dayton and his wife Mary Lee gave a dinner for her at the Minneapolis Club, and the next day the group flew the 76-year-old woman over the proposed preserve in a private plane, then drove her all over it in a pickup truck. Barnard collected prairie plants for her and found that she knew them well. At one point the party spotted a nest in the grass with a clutch of small eggs in it, and one larger egg, clearly a cowbird's (female cowbirds lay eggs in the nests of other species, thus neatly delegating the work of hatching and feeding their young; the smaller host's eggs or young are frequently destroyed by the cowbird mother or its young). A lengthy debate ensued, while the professional preservationists discussed whether to remove the cowbird egg to save the others or, in keeping with the philosophy of their occupation, to let nature take its course. The discussion ended when Kay Ordway reached down with a frail hand, picked up the parasite egg, and hurled it as far as she could. As Roush saw it, "she was tidying up her prairie."

The day was a success. Wally Dayton got one of the rare photographs that Katharine Ordway would allow to be taken of her — in slacks, with her inevitable umbrella to ward off the sun, inspecting the plants that Barnard had found for her. More important, she confirmed that she would fund the purchase, to establish the Samuel H. Ordway, Jr., Memorial Prairie. At the dedication of the preserve that September, Noonan called it "the jewel in the Ordway Prairie System" and "one of the hallmark purchases in the Conservancy's history."

Some months later, Barnard sent Miss Ordway a photograph newly taken on the preserve by a freelance photographer named Jim Brandenburg, to commemorate the day and the dedication of the outstanding new prairie sanctuary. It was a dramatic close-up of a ferruginous hawk with upraised wings, alighting on the edge of its nest in the needlegrass to defend its four downy white chicks. The picture was to become widely known and heavily used by Conservancy staff and volunteers, for its life and beauty and for its symbolism, the ferruginous hawk being dependent for its nesting and hunting grounds on native prairie, as humanity depends for its survival on the global natural environment, and disappearing as the prairie itself disappears.

Within two years, two of the largest wildlife species that had been extirpated from the area had been reintroduced on the new Ordway preserve: the giant race of Canada goose, biggest of its subspecies, and the bison.

Meanwhile, important events were occurring elsewhere. Lloyd Hulbert and The Nature Conservancy had both been keeping an eye on the bigger property next door to their Konza preserve — a property known as the Dewey Ranch, for the family that had assembled it in the 19th century. In 1975, after earlier efforts to acquire adjoining tracts had fallen through, the Conservancy opened negotiations with the current owner, a Manhattan (Kansas) physician, David McKnight. But the talks dragged on into 1976, and the price kept rising. Katharine Ordway grew tired of waiting and presented an ultimatum. Make a deal in 48 hours, she told the Conservancy, "or the money goes to Planned Parenthood."

Barnard and the Conservancy's general counsel, John R. Flicker, boarded planes for one more trip to Kansas and an all-day session with McKnight. At the end of the day, they had a deal. The Conservancy would swap land in Oklahoma, costing $3.6 million, for 7,220 acres of the Dewey Ranch. Said Flicker: "Miss Ordway applied the pressure just when we needed it."

The new addition stretched a full three miles north from the original site, to the floodplain of the Kansas River — a spectacular sweep of Flint Hills upland prairie broken by wooded draws and drainageways, only six miles from

Kansas State University. More than 25 species of grasses and grass-like plants could be found there, with more than 200 species of other plants. The native grazing herds and the wolves that preyed on them were gone, and the coyote was now at the head of the food chain, but the potential for reintroduction was there.

The deal closed in January of 1977, and in December of that year the Conservancy bid successfully in a sealed-bid auction for 480 acres more of adjoining good prairie to improve the western boundary of the reserve. Now the preserve managers at the university and their 19-member scientific advisory committee (two Conservancy representatives, nine university faculty members, and eight other scientists from as far away as Georgia and California) could start to plan in earnest for studies involving the native grazers in comparison with domestic stock.

Here at last was the really big tallgrass prairie preserve that Katharine Ordway had wanted to see — the sea of high grass in all directions, with no man-made interruptions as far as the eye could see. With a major prairie research center, to boot. She had given nearly $4 million, in all, to acquire the land. It was to be the climax of her personal preservation work. Ironically, and sadly, she was never to see it herself.

Her policy had been to visit all her prairies when she could, before she was committed to their purchase, especially the larger ones. But she had become increasingly frail and accident-prone with age, and there were other problems. In the spring of 1977 the university had wanted to celebrate the enlargement of the preserve with a banquet in her honor. She had wanted to go, to see the prairie with its flowers in bloom, but then her identity as the donor of the land, hitherto a secret, had leaked to the press. Worse, a crank threat against her life had been sent to a newspaper. Her advisors counseled caution, and she passed up the banquet, hoping for a quiet visit later in the year. Instead, she had another fall, with a broken pelvis and a long recuperation. Time was running out.

For Lloyd Hulbert, who had become the first director of what was formally named the Konza Prairie Research Natural Area, the preserve was the realization of a decades-old dream. The tallgrass prairie research center was a

*Above: Lloyd C. Hulbert, a biologist at Kansas State University, headed the faculty team that identified the tract later called Konza as one of the two finest large tallgrass sites remaining in the state. Following the Ordway purchases there, he became the first director of the Konza Prairie Research Natural Area; and it became one of the first sites chosen by the National Science Foundation for long-term ecological research.*

fact, and it had the largest protected tallgrass prairie in the country as its outdoor laboratory. Almost none of its land had ever been plowed. There was no road through it. Some cattle had grazed there, but the native plants were largely undisturbed. For all these reasons and others, Konza soon became one of the first six sites chosen by the National Science Foundation for long-term ecological research. And in 1979, the United Nations recognized Konza through the UNESCO Man and the Biosphere Program by designating it an International Biosphere Reserve, part of a global system of protected examples of the world's major ecosystems dedicated to conservation and scientific research.

"Our major goal," Hulbert wrote, "is understanding the forces and processes that make the tallgrass prairie a long-lasting system," to help us improve our management of grassland, water and wildlife.

"Our treatment of forests, rangelands and soils . . . has been a bit like the furniture manufacturer who tore down his factory to obtain the lumber to build furniture. Without ample resources of reasonable cost, our standard of living will markedly decline. A great need now is to learn how to make the benefits [of our natural resources] sustainable in the future. It is a multi-faceted task. Our part is to understand natural forces so we can work in harmony with, not against them. A major goal of the work on Konza Prairie is to develop such understanding."

By 1987 an initial ten miles of 15-wire fence had been completed, on 12-foot posts sunk four feet into the ground, to keep in elk and pronghorn. To keep bison from leaning on the fence and breaking it or from just plain bulling their way through, it was mildly electrified. Then the first of the reintroduced native grazers arrived: a small herd of buffalo. But that was a decade after the land purchase, and by then both Kay Ordway and Hulbert were gone.

After Konza, the tempo of acquisition slowed for the prairie system. In 1978, recovered from her fall, Katharine Ordway visited the Conservancy's Virginia Coast Reserve, where since 1969, with the help primarily of the Mary Flagler Cary Charitable Trust of New York, the organization had been building a major preserve — an entire barrier island chain, stretching over 40 miles along the Atlantic coast. Noonan had taken her there once before, in 1974, for a day's boat trip through the islands and marshes. She thought the marshes reminiscent of the prairie, with their expanses of waving green, stirred by wind and tide, and she had added coastal marshes to her list of priorities for the Goodhill Foundation. Now she agreed to help the Conservancy buy a property at Brownsville, Virginia, on the Eastern Shore mainland, to serve as a headquarters site for the big preserve.

She had wanted for years to do something to express her admiration and gratitude for Dick Pough. She had hinted to him that she would like to leave him a substantial gift, which he had discouraged. Now she decided on an alternative. The Nature Conservancy was conducting a $20-million capital fund drive for its revolving fund to buy land; she was contributing $1.3 million to it — $1 million for prairies and $300,000 for the Brownsville headquarters site. Now she decided to add another $1 million in Pough's name, for a Richard H. Pough Land Preservation Fund, as an indication of her regard.

The Nature Conservancy was thinking about recognition, too: how to recognize Katharine Ordway?

Two years earlier, discussing fund raising with Noonan, Miss Ordway had suggested creating a new category of major donors to the Conservancy, to be called "guardians." She liked the concept of guarding the land. Now the Conservancy decided to act on her suggestion, but to reshape it. Instead, the organization created a new award, an honor to be conferred from time to time on one person only, and for life, for services of unique dimensions, with the title of "The Land Guardian." Preparations were in progress for months. A large, specially designed gold pin was ordered from Tiffany & Co., in New York, in the shape of an oak leaf — the Conservancy emblem — and inscribed on the back, "#1 K.O. Land Guardian." It was to be accompanied by an illuminated parchment certificate.

After plans for a formal presentation at a lunch in New York had to be postponed, Noonan flew out to Tucson, where the honoree was wintering, to join Wally Dayton in making a small private presentation (Dayton was to succeed to the honor eight years later himself). Kay Ordway received the news, and the gifts, with tears in her eyes. Later, Noonan carried the framed scroll back east,

# The Board of Governors

of

# The Nature Conservancy

confers for life
the honors and title
of

# THE LAND GUARDIAN

upon

# Katharine Ordway

This singular action carries with it all the joys and responsibilities
of enduring membership and is given in grateful acknowledge-
ment of her commitment to the preservation of Native
American prairies and in appreciative recognition of her
dedication to the protection of the natural world and
the rich variety of life it shelters.
Given this 25th day of March, 1978

John E. Andrus, III
Chairman.

Patrick F. Noonan
President.

to save her the inconvenience, and six weeks later it was formally re-presented to her at the postponed lunch in New York, by Conservancy Chairman John Andrus. The certificate read:

*The Board of Governors of The Nature Conservancy confers for life the honors and title of The Land Guardian upon Katharine Ordway. This singular action...is given in grateful acknowledgment of her commitment to the preservation of native American prairies and in appreciative recognition of her dedication to the protection of the natural world and the rich variety of life it shelters.*

A framed photo of the scroll was presented to Ray Carter, in thanks for his unfailing help. Carter was later to buy the pin from Kay Ordway's estate as a memento of his long-time client and to present it publicly to his wife, Augusta, at a Conservancy gathering at which he was honored, in appreciation of her partnership in all his efforts, including his support for Miss Ordway.

In the ensuing months, her last, Katharine Ordway was thinking beyond her death. She renewed and updated her instructions to the Goodhill Foundation and confirmed her will, which was to create one last, personally selected, refuge: her home place at Weston. Businesslike as ever, she directed that the house and 11 acres around it were to be sold by The Nature Conservancy to endow the refuge, and she left $100,000 in cash for the same purpose. The remaining 61 acres of mixed hardwood forest, undisturbed for nearly a century, with her arboretum and some fields in various stages of reforestation were to become a Conservancy preserve — the Katharine Ordway Preserve, her own.

Her art collection was to go to Yale, and $1 million to the University of Minnesota Foundation for a scholarship fund. After smaller gifts to a number of relatives, friends, and employees, the bulk of her estate was left to her foundation.

*Opposite: The Nature Conservancy found it difficult to conceive of an adequate expression of gratitude and admiration for Katharine Ordway's extraordinary contribution to natural-area conservation. In 1978, a year before her death, the organization created for her a special honor — a title, to be held for life, by her only. As this scroll testified, to the Conservancy she was now "The Land Guardian."*

Predictably, everything was in order when the stroke felled her, in May 1979, during her annual stay in the Arizona desert. Ray Carter rushed out from New York and flew her back in a chartered plane. She lingered for weeks in the Cornell New York Hospital. Noonan was among her frequent visitors, but he couldn't be sure she recognized him. On June 27 she died, at the age of 80.

By her own wish, there was no funeral service. Instead, she wanted her ashes returned to the land, on her favorite hillside.

At Ray Carter's invitation, a small group gathered on the Weston property one day in July, and later Carter and Noonan walked along her favorite path. Carter opened a container and, with Noonan's help, began to scatter its contents. As he later recorded it, in his lawyerly way, in a memo for his file, he then commented:

*Our dear Miss Katharine Ordway had the opportunity which few mortals possess to provide so unselfishly for the welfare of her fellow beings . . . . she left this world a better place in which to live — including Weston, Fairfield County, the Prairie areas of the mid-West, and the Virginia shoreline . . . . Miss Ordway, I have now complied with your last wish. You will forever be a part of this beautiful and particular area which you have directed to be preserved as open space.*

*May God have mercy on your soul.*

This time it was Carter and Noonan who had tears in their eyes. Years later, Noonan recalled that "when she died, a bit of light in my life went out. It was a very emotional moment for me, that whole time. I couldn't believe she was going to pass away. It helped to convince me that my time had come to leave" — as president of The Nature Conservancy, which he did within a year, after seven highly successful years in that position.

Katharine Ordway was gone. She had given more than $12 million for the land, nearly all of it to The Nature Conservancy. But her contribution to natural-area preservation in a sense had just begun.

*Five who helped: from the left, Clifford E. Emanuelson, who proposed the Devil's Den sanctuary and became its first director; Patrick F. Noonan, president of The Nature Conservancy 1973–80; Ann Moore, wife of Frederick Moore, Miss Ordway's caretaker at Weston and later manager of the Katharine Ordway Preserve there; Pough, and Raymond A. Carter, Kay Ordway's lawyer for many years. Fred Moore took the picture.*

# Critical Areas &
# Endangered Species

*Above: Leadplant*

*Overleaf: Pure streams watering semidesert forest and grassland communities in the canyons of Arizona's Galiuro Mountains made the Muleshoe Ranch a "critical area" for preservation.*

*WHEN THE ORDWAY ESTATE* had been settled, the Goodhill Foundation share turned out to be more than $40 million. But with capital appreciation, income, and good management, the foundation in the end was to have nearly $53 million to distribute over the remaining five years of its life.

Goodhill had been set up for Katharine Ordway in 1959 by Ray Carter, with the donor as president and a nephew, John G. Ordway, Jr., and a niece, Dorothy Ordway Mills, as well as cousin Sam, among the initial directors. But Kay Ordway never made much use of Goodhill in her lifetime. Over the 20 years before her death, the foundation gave away less than $800,000; at the end, she was donating directly $1 million to $2 million a year. She enjoyed making the gifts; "she had the joy of giving more than anyone I've ever known," Noonan said. Carter believed she would have liked to give it all away, quietly, during her lifetime, if she could have done so in an orderly and thoughtful way. She soon came to see the foundation as a vehicle for giving away after her death what she hadn't been able to distribute herself while she lived.

As early as 1969, Kay Ordway had indicated to the foundation board that there would be substantial funds remaining at her death and that she wanted them spent "within a reasonable time thereafter." A year later she circulated a written statement to the directors: "I do not wish the Foundation to continue its operation indefinitely. It would be my hope that projects could be found within a reasonable time after my death and that the principal and income of the Foundation be fully expended for the purposes mentioned" — namely, "acquiring land for conservation." These instructions were reconfirmed more or less annually at the directors' meetings until her death.

In accordance with her priorities, the bulk of the $778,000 distributed by Goodhill before her death had been given, mostly in small amounts, for conservation, and more than half of the total had gone to The Nature Conservancy.

At the time of Kay Ordway's death, there were three other directors. One was her nephew Jack (also known as "Smokey") Ordway, a board member from the beginning and now vice president of the foundation, whom his aunt had long respected for his business judgment. Chairman and majority stockholder of the MacArthur Company in St. Paul, which handled distribution and contracting of construction specialty products, he was an outdoorsman, fisherman, and sailor. He was later to play the key role in protecting from development a wild river in northern Wisconsin, the Brule, where the family owned property. With Ray Carter and the Bank of New York, he was also an executor of Kay Ordway's estate.

Carter himself had become a Goodhill director in 1969, following Dorothy Mills's withdrawal. He had been Kay Ordway's lawyer since Samuel Ordway had introduced him to her in the mid-1950s and had been intimately involved in the legal and financial arrangements for all of her projects with the Conservancy. His best-known client had been the financier Bernard M. Baruch, advisor to presidents and author of the Baruch Plan for international control of atomic energy. Sharing Kay Ordway's birthday (April 3) but eight years her junior, Carter had continued as an active partner in his New York law firm while his principal client lived. With her death, he retired at age 72 to "of counsel" status with the firm but continued to manage the foundation from his office. A resident of Pound Ridge, New York, he had been an early chairman of the planning board there and had supervised the enactment of innovative back-lot development regulations, which were predecessors of one of the first town development plans.

The third remaining board member at her death was her long-time conservation counselor and friend Dick Pough, who had retired as president of the Open Space Institute five years earlier but was still very much active at age 75 as conservation matchmaker and president of the Natural Areas Council.

These three were to be responsible for the Goodhill Foundation's affairs until the foundation dissolved, an event which they quickly decided should occur within five years, in the spirit of the founder's instructions. Jack Ordway was asked to succeed his aunt as president but declined, saying the chief officer should be based in New York; so Pough was elected president with Ordway as vice president, and Carter continued to manage the daily business as secretary and counsel. The Bank of New York served as appointed treasurer and investment advisor.

In the beginning, the three-man board went at its task on a project-by-project basis, as Katharine Ordway had done. Recognizing her interest in The Nature Conservancy's Virginia Coast Reserve, the directors immediately approved an additional $900,000 grant for acquisitions on three islands in the 18-island chain, 13 of which were now wholly or partly under Conservancy protection, with two others protected by state and federal government. There was no other such protected barrier-island chain in the country, if indeed one existed anywhere. Like Konza, this refuge was to become a United Nations Biosphere Reserve.

The directors also promptly approved a $3 million challenge grant to help establish a preserve at Mashomack Point on Shelter Island, at the eastern end of Long Island, New York. In an unusual preservation tactic, the Conservancy was buying out the Aeon Realty Corporation for $10.6 million and selling off its other assets from New York to Florida, to acquire Aeon's holding of one-third of Shelter Island — more than 2,000 acres of wilderness, with ten miles of beaches, tidal marshes and creeks, and oak woodland. The property embraced colonies of ibis, herons, egrets, and terns, and one of the largest nesting areas for fish hawks on the Atlantic coast, all within 100 miles of New York City. After sale of the unwanted assets, including brownstone houses in New York and warehouses in Florida, the Conservancy's cost for the reserve would be around $6 million, including $1 million in start-up management costs.

Confirming the Goodhill grant, Carter wrote to Bradford C. Northrup, Conservancy vice president for the Eastern region:

*Miss Ordway owned for almost twenty years prior to her death and occupied a waterfront summer home in Bridgehampton, Long Island. The trustees believe that she would have wished to help preserve Mashomack's 2,000-acre parcel of salt marshes and forest so near to her loved eight-acre property.*

In what was to become a pattern for Goodhill-Conservancy relations, the matching requirement of the grant was quickly met, with major help from the

Richard King Mellon Foundation of Pittsburgh. Some 1,500 people and organizations contributed to what was then the most successful project fund-raising campaign the Conservancy had ever mounted.

The next year, 1980, was a year of tremendous accomplishment for the Goodhill Foundation, now in charge of major resources and with a deadline to meet for distributing them. It began with a lunch-table discussion between Ray Carter and Robert Marston, president of the University of Florida, who had a proposal to make. Carter had graduated from the university and its law school in the 1930s and had practiced law in Florida for two years before moving to New York.

In 1975 The Nature Conservancy had accepted a memorial gift of nearly 3,000 acres in northern Florida, east of Gainesville, from the widow of the late Carl S. Swisher, a cigar manufacturer and fishing enthusiast. The property contained unpolluted lakes, marsh, cypress swamp, grassland, and scrub oak upland — habitat for a number of threatened species, including red-cockaded woodpeckers, Florida sandhill cranes, southern bald eagles, and the eastern indigo snake. To support its research programs in water supply (increasingly critical in north central Florida) and other subjects, the university now proposed to buy an adjoining 6,145 acres of sandhills and scrub forest dotted with lakes and to lease the original tract from the Conservancy at $1 a year, to create a 9,000-acre outdoor laboratory. The university also proposed to set up a Katharine Ordway Teaching Chair in Ecosystem Conservation, in part with state funds. In all, it was asking for $5.2 million from Goodhill for these purposes.

The proposal was welcomed by the Conservancy — Florida scrub was a vanishing system — and by all the Goodhill directors, and the land purchase

*Opposite: Ocean beaches and dunes at The Nature Conservancy's Virginia Coast Reserve, a 40-mile chain of barrier islands and marshes. Miss Ordway helped to buy a headquarters site for it on the mainland (see pages 100–101). After her death, the Goodhill Foundation, which she had established and funded, continued to support land acquisition for the unique preserve.*

closed in July. "This land is as virgin as you can find in Florida today," commented the director of the Florida State Museum.

At the end of May the foundation announced what was believed to be the largest single cash contribution ever made for a private conservation project: nearly $11 million, to purchase 54,000 acres of prairie and forest along 22 miles of the Niobrara River, in northern Nebraska. Three types of prairie — sandhill, mixed-grass, and tallgrass — met here with eastern, western, and northern forest types: stands of eastern deciduous hardwoods such as bur oak, basswood, ironwood, and black walnut adjoining stands of mountain conifers such as ponderosa pine, at its easternmost reach, and paper birch, hundreds of miles from its normal range to the north. In areas of ecosystem and species overlap like this, scientists say, hybridization is fostered and the pace of evolution quickened. Ice Age mammal fossils had been found along the river valley, at the center of the historic range of the more recent plains bison. A large prairie dog town remained.

When the Conservancy first proposed buying this huge property, the Goodhill trustees hesitated. It was too much; there would have to be funding from other sources, for a match. And there was also a threat of flooding by the Norden Dam, a long-planned, long-delayed Bureau of Reclamation dam project on the Niobrara. But the Conservancy was skeptical of the prospects for local fund raising, and with only one rough access road to the ranch headquarters and little other sign of man, the property met Kay Ordway's desire to protect really big expanses of prairie. Biologists and paleontologists were pressing for its protection; so were the many recreational users of nearly the last long stretch of wild river on the Great Plains.

*Opposite: Southern bald eagles (shown here) and other threatened species, such as red-cockaded woodpeckers, gopher tortoises, and eastern indigo snakes, are found at the Ordway–Swisher Preserve in northern Florida, where Kay Ordway's foundation and the University of Florida, with help from The Nature Conservancy, joined to create a 9,000-acre refuge and ecological laboratory.*

*At the dedication of the Konza Prairie Research Natural Area, Kansas, 1980: from the left, the three Goodhill Foundation directors, Raymond Carter, Richard Pough, and John G. Ordway, Jr., Katharine's nephew and business counselor; and the author.*

In early May the Goodhill directors visited Konza for its dedication, then flew by chartered plane to Valentine, Nebraska, to look at the Niobrara tract. They canoed a stretch of the river and camped above it overnight. Ten days later they met again at Conservancy headquarters in Arlington, Virginia, to review the proposal. The meeting was interrupted for lunch with Secretary of the Interior Cecil D. Andrus, who congratulated them on the important work for the nation that they had helped Katharine Ordway to do, and were still doing. After lunch, the trustees reconvened in Arlington and voted to go for it all.

Over the next several years, the dam threat was to be first put off and then removed by congressional action after a long campaign involving local members of Congress, a local Save the Niobrara Association, the National Taxpayers' Association, the Water Conservation Council, and many others — a campaign orchestrated in part by John Flicker of The Nature Conservancy. Studies during the campaign found that the costs of the dam would far outweigh the benefits, and that the purposes of the dam could be served better and cheaper by other means.

By 1985 bison had been returned to the preserve, and within two years numbered more than 100.

Two months after the trustees' decision on Niobrara and five days after the Florida closing, the Conservancy and Goodhill announced another big buy: 23,605 acres of sedge, rush, and tule marsh, wet grassland, and pine forest in Lake and Klamath Counties, south-central Oregon, the Conservancy's largest project in the Northwest at that time. The mile-high wetlands, bought for $5 million, were an important link on the Pacific Flyway; a major nesting area for greater sandhill cranes, with an estimated 250 breeding pairs; and habitat for a number of other threatened species, including the long-billed curlew, great gray owls, and goshawks and a rich variety of plant life. The refuge was named the Katharine Ordway Sycan Marsh Preserve.

Two weeks after that announcement, the Goodhill trustees were on the road again, to West Palm Beach, Florida, where they met with senior staff of both the Conservancy and the National Audubon Society. The next day, July 25, the group drove 90 miles northwest past Lake Okeechobee to the vicinity of Fort Drum and the Kissimmee River, to inspect what was believed to be the best and perhaps the last sizeable remnant of unaltered "palmetto prairie" — a grassland interspersed with palmetto clumps — in existence. Most of the original two million acres of that system had been destroyed or severely degraded by truck farming, cattle grazing, and other uses. Now the two conservation organizations cooperatively proposed to buy 6,000 acres of it for $3.5 million, of which Audubon would put up $1 million from an earlier legacy (from a benefactor named George Whittell), as a preserve and site for an Audubon Nature Center.

Would Goodhill put up the other $2.5 million? It would, and did. The purchase established the Ordway–Whittell Kissimmee Prairie, in an area where Dick Pough had led natural history tours 30 years before and where caracara (birds of prey related to the hawks and falcons), burrowing owls, mottled duck, bobcat, and other increasingly uncommon fauna were still found. Audubon later added another 1,600 acres to the sanctuary.

Hardly pausing to draw breath, the Goodhill trustees then made a further grant of $1 million to the National Audubon Society in October, to protect the entire shoreline of Alkali Lake in the pothole country of southeastern North Dakota, near Jamestown.

But the most important was yet to come. Walking the Niobrara sandhills with their Conservancy escorts, the trustees had posed a provocative question: among all the different types of natural areas, or ecosystems, or plant and animal communities, which were The Nature Conservancy's highest priorities for protection? Which were the nation's?

The Conservancy had been working on an answer to that precise question. Under the leadership of Robert E. Jenkins, a young biologist who had joined the staff as ecology advisor in 1970 and become vice president for science two years later, the first statewide inventory of the "natural heritage" had been launched in South Carolina in 1974. Jenkins's brainchild was a systematic program to collect, map, and computerize the existing data on all the natural systems and species known or suspected to be threatened with extinction in the inventory area; to identify needs for further information and to supply it through new field work; and to analyze the findings to develop preservation priorities and a protection program. By 1980 the Conservancy had organized Natural Heritage (inventory) Programs in nearly half the states, normally in cooperation with state agencies; but the network was still far from the nationwide resource, the most comprehensive of its kind, that it was to have become a few years later. Neither the Conservancy nor any other authority in May 1980 had an up-to-date and reasonably complete national assessment of endangered natural systems. The Goodhill trustees' question was very much to the point.

The Conservancy rose to the challenge. Drawing on every available source — academia, government, other organizations, and individual experts — Jenkins and his department launched a crash effort to form a truly national overview.

The preliminary results were disturbing. "We found that the loss of entire major American ecosystems — something conservationists have warned about for much of this century — is actually occurring," Executive Vice President L. Gregory Low reported in *The Nature Conservancy News* for January and February 1981. "In fact, the Conservancy has been unable to locate a single recognizable or undamaged example of several ecosystems, the Mississippi–Alabama blackbelt savanna [grassland with scattered trees] and certain lowland Hawaiian forest types among them."

Many of the natural-area types found in grave danger of eradication were grasslands, like Katharine Ordway's beloved tallgrass prairie. Others were aquatic and riparian systems. They included unchanged watercourses and streambank woodlands of the dry Southwest; fragile scrub systems of the desert; the bottomland forest swamps of the Southeast — systems hard hit by development of all kinds but largely passed over by conservation efforts tending to favor spectacular scenery.

In California alone, 11 unprotected systems on the verge of extinction were identified, from wetlands covered by vernal pools, which disappear in summer, to the old-growth Douglas-fir forests of the coastal mountains.

By October of 1980, the overall picture was clear enough to support the Conservancy's basic conclusion and a proposal to the Goodhill Foundation for strong action. "There is a clear and present need to launch a major private initiative to protect America's most endangered natural lands," the proposal began. "Unfortunately, government land acquisition funds are being cut just as pressures to permanently alter America's natural landscape are reaching an all-time high. Whole ecosystem types not now protected may be lost forever, and with them a wealth of scientific knowledge and applied uses that can never be recovered."

It was time to aim high. The Conservancy proposed a three-year, $30-million National Critical Areas Conservation Program, to save areas at the very top of the preservation priority list. And it asked Goodhill for a $10-million challenge grant for the program, which the Conservancy would match two for one (i.e., by raising $20 million for the program from other sources).

The Goodhill directors deliberated and agreed.

To promote energetic fund raising and to get the maximum effect from every Goodhill dollar, the Conservancy encouraged its units across the country to "bid" for the Goodhill funds — to offer the biggest match they thought they could make in return for a share of the grant for their projects. Allowance was made for the limited fund-raising capabilities of poorer areas with fewer people, fewer foundations, and fewer large corporate givers. As a result of this practice, in most of the "critical area" projects Katharine Ordway's dollars tended to represent half or less of the total spent — often much less. Her "leverage," in the jargon of finance and philanthropy, was great.

The Goodhill directors reviewed each project in advance on the basis of a detailed fact sheet from the Conservancy, and of a personal visit in some cases. The projects ranged from New York to Hawaii and from a small desert wetland in New Mexico to a rare Atlantic maritime forest in the dunes of the Outer Banks of North Carolina. In all, more than 40 projects received Goodhill help under this program, and some of these were actually aggregations of projects in themselves, like the California Critical Areas Program or the Rivers of the Deep South, the two largest beneficiaries.

The Rivers of the Deep South project was a $30-million, five-year undertaking to preserve 350,000 acres of the bottomland hardwood forest along major Southern rivers, from the Pearl in Louisiana to the Suwannee in Florida. This swamp-forest system of the Southeast, important to the region's water supply, flood control, fisheries nourishment, and recreation, once covered 50 million acres. But by 1980 it had shrunk to 3.5 million and was disappearing at a rate of 300,000 acres a year, mostly through conversion for agriculture. The effort to preserve it, conceived and directed by David E. Morine, Conservancy vice president for land acquisition, was to be funded in part by a record $15-million grant from the Richard King Mellon Foundation; the Conservancy had pledged to raise another $15 million for it. One million dollars of the Goodhill grant was allocated to launch this campaign. Most of the large tracts acquired were to be turned over to state and federal conservation agencies to protect and manage as natural areas.

Through the California Critical Areas Program, the Conservancy sought to preserve one good example of each of the 11 natural systems in California that had been found to be in danger of total elimination. Wetland, grassland, and forest types were included with others in a $15-million drive, to which $1.5 million of the Ordway funds was assigned as a challenge to be met — as it was — by raising $9 from other donors for every $1 of the grant.

Some of the other best-known projects in the National Critical Areas Conservation Program were the following:

*PINE BUTTE SWAMP, MONTANA.* Another $1 million of the Goodhill grant went to the first phase of a continuing, multi-million-dollar effort to protect 40,000 acres along the Rocky Mountain front in Montana, centered on the only high plains swamp habitat remaining in the lower 48 states, by acquisition and easement. Wildlife including the grizzly, wolf, lynx, and mountain goat is abundant here.

*Twilight on the Ordway–Whittell Kissimmee Prairie, a last big tract of "palmetto prairie" in northern Florida. The reserve provides habitat for the rare burrowing owl (above) and other increasingly uncommon species of wildlife. Goodhill helped the National Aubudon Society to acquire the land as a sanctuary and nature center site.*

*HAWAIIAN FOREST, THE HAWAIIAN ISLANDS.* The most isolated land mass on Earth, this is one of the world's great centers of endemism — of plant and animal species found nowhere else. Hawaii's forest-dwelling honeycreepers, if less celebrated, are an even more startling example of evolutionary radiation than Darwin's famous finches of the Galapagos Islands. In Hawaii more than 20 and perhaps as many as 47 species of honeycreepers may have evolved from a single ancestral bird species. But the destruction of their forest habitat urgently threatens their continued existence: of around 70 endemic species of birds living there when Captain Cook arrived, two centuries ago, more than 50 are today either extinct or in imminent danger of extinction. Accordingly, $1 million of the Goodhill challenge went to spark a $3-million campaign to enlarge the Hawaiian network of protected koa and 'ohi'a forest lands.

*HONEY CREEK, TEXAS.* The Conservancy allocated $1 million more to help protect a 1,825-acre juniper–live oak savanna along a creek flowing down to the Guadalupe River, with a mixture of grasses found only in this area on the Edwards Plateau. Rare golden-cheeked warblers nest in the juniper, and two of the native fish species in the creek are also found only on the plateau.

*MULESHOE RANCH, ARIZONA.* In this project, aided by $625,000 of the Ordway funds, purchase of private land and leases of state- and federally owned lands combined to build a 51,000-acre preserve across the southern end of the Galiuro Mountains. Its rocky canyons and rugged cliffs, part of the historic range of the desert bighorn sheep, bound several entire watersheds, with some of the last unpolluted and uninvaded (by non-native species) ever-flowing streams in southern Arizona. Among other increasingly uncommon species found here are black, gray, and zone-tailed hawks, beardless flycatchers, and Arizona cypress trees.

*CROSS RANCH, NORTH DAKOTA.* More than 6,400 people, or 1 percent of the population of North Dakota, contributed money to save this 5,000-acre parcel of mixed-grass and floodplain prairie with riparian woodland along eight miles of the Missouri River northwest of Bismarck. The Goodhill grant provided a $400,000 challenge to boost the $3-million campaign.

*NAGS HEAD WOODS, NORTH CAROLINA.* One of the rarest of the natural areas protected under the Critical Areas Program was this ancient and now nearly unique maritime forest, complete with freshwater ponds and swamps, in the back barrier dunes of the Outer Banks within sight of the Atlantic Ocean. The Goodhill Foundation gave more than $500,000 in challenge grants to help save 610 acres of it from recreation-home development, at a total cost of over $2 million.

The dozens of other projects helped by the National Critical Areas Conservation Program were generally smaller and received smaller allocations.

In May 1982 the national Board of Governors of The Nature Conservancy held its quarterly meeting in San Antonio, Texas. There, the Conservancy's director of development, J. Mason Morfit, reported to the Development Committee of the board that the organization was just $210.06 short of meeting the $20-million Goodhill matching requirement. Passing the hat to the board and staff members present in the room, he collected the shortfall on the spot.

The Conservancy had met the big three-year challenge in 18 months. By that date, it had also brought 138,000 acres of increasingly rare and threatened types of natural area under permanent protection, with much of the Goodhill funding remaining to be committed. Katharine Ordway's legacy, and her priorities, had been the energizing factor in the program's success.

With the unprecedented challenge met, the Conservancy could look for a new one from the same source, and it did.

The loss of different plant and animal life forms to total extinction, in the United States as well as globally, was continuing at a rapid and accelerating pace. The federal government's Endangered Species Program, the Conservancy's president wrote to the Goodhill directors, was itself "virtually extinct, for lack of funding." In the previous two years it had managed to list just one species for special protection under the Endangered Species Act, out of hundreds proposed for such protection.

The Conservancy was proposing a new, private, endangered species program — a three-year, $15-million effort, which it asked the Goodhill Foundation once again to set in motion with a big challenge grant, this time of $5 million,

*Opposite: The rapid decline of Hawaii's unique woodland birds, including this 'amakihi honeycreeper, targeted their shrinking forest habitat for urgent protection with the help of the National Critical Areas Conservation Program. The program was launched with a $10-million challenge grant from the Goodhill Foundation, to be matched at least two for one in dollars from other sources.*

with the Conservancy to raise $10 million from other sources to earn it. (It was felt that with the focus directly on species, rather than on ecosystems and natural communities of species, preserve size on the average would be smaller, and cost lower, than in the Critical Areas Program.)

"No one else has so intensively researched the real endangerment status of our flora and fauna as we have, through our state Natural Heritage inventories and otherwise," the president wrote. Through the proposed new program, over three years, "we hope to safeguard 100 to 150 of the most endangered species (e.g., the masked bobwhite, the Florida manatee, a number of rare wildflowers) by assuring them at least a minimum of critical habitat in 75 to 150 new preserves . . . .

"We believe an effective national endangered species conservation program to be the most important biological conservation effort remaining to be launched in the 1980s."

The Goodhill Foundation approved, and the Katharine Ordway Endangered Species Conservation Program was launched. It was conducted similarly to the earlier effort. The Ordway funds were allocated on a challenge basis to more than 60 campaigns mounted by Conservancy units across the country, some of those campaigns financing the establishment of not just one but a number of new preserves.

The following are representative of the scores of new refuges that were created in campaigns sparked by the Endangered Species Program:

HAWAIIAN "ISLANDS OF LIFE." In the only seven-figure grant under this program, the Conservancy allocated $1 million to a $10-million Hawaiian drive under this name to establish eight new reserves, with the Mo'omomi Dunes on Molokai as the centerpiece — the least altered remaining refuge for

*Opposite: The 2,800-acre Kamakou Preserve on the island of Molokai was established with Goodhill support to save outstanding examples of several different Hawaiian forest and bog communities with their rare plant and bird life. The all but extinct Hawaiian thrush, or Molokai oloma'o, and other endemic birds inhabit the preserve.*

Hawaiian coastal vegetation, with at least five close-to-extinction native plant species and an area that the Hawaiian green sea turtle, extirpated on the main islands, was now attempting to recolonize.

*ASH MEADOWS, NEVADA.* Twelve major spring systems combine here to form the largest oasis in the Mojave Desert. The area supports more than 20 species found nowhere else on Earth, including the Devil's Hole pupfish and a number of invertebrates and plants, the greatest concentration of endemic species in so small an area in the continental United States. With the help of $500,000 from the Goodhill grant for the multi-million-dollar project, the Conservancy acquired 13,000 key acres and turned them over to the U.S. Fish and Wildlife Service to become a national wildlife refuge.

*CRYSTAL RIVER, FLORIDA.* This river on the west coast of Florida north of Tampa is the wintering ground for one of the largest remaining populations of the declining West Indian manatee — more than 120 animals, or around 10 percent of the known North American population at the time. After two years of quiet negotiation, the Conservancy bought 14 undeveloped and much-desired islands in King's Bay on the river, at the heart of the wintering ground, to maintain the habitat and become part of the Crystal River Manatee Sanctuary, under lease to the U.S. Fish and Wildlife Service. Of the Goodhill challenge, $50,000 went into this $425,000 project.

*MOBILE–TENSAW DELTA WILDLIFE MANAGEMENT AREA, ALABAMA.* This was an 18,000-acre refuge established by the Coastal Land Trust of Mobile with Nature Conservancy help, including $250,000 from the Goodhill grant.

*PENDLETON ISLAND, VIRGINIA.* In one of the smallest of the Endangered Species Program projects, three wooded islets in the Clinch River in southwestern Virginia were protected with their adjacent riffles, pools, and shoals to preserve one of the world's richest arrays of freshwater mollusks in one place — more than 50 species, at least ten of them rare and threatened. The Goodhill contribution to this 35-acre undertaking was just $5,000.

*SAVANNAH RIVER BLUFFS, SOUTH CAROLINA.* The 110 acres of bluffs and ravines acquired here sheltered a list of increasingly uncommon to rare plants,

On the west coast of Florida at King's Bay, on the Crystal River, the Goodhill
Foundation helped to save 14 islands from development that would have threatened the
wintering ground for about 10 percent of the known North American population of
manatees (above). This was a project of the Katharine Ordway Endangered Species
Conservation Program.

among them relict and lance-leaved trillium, bottlebrush buckeye, yellowwood, and false rue anemone. The Goodhill allocation was $144,000.

*THOUSAND PALMS OASIS, CALIFORNIA.* A desert wetland on the San Andreas Fault with a fine stand of desert fan palms, this area formed the heart of the Conservancy's Coachella Valley Preserve. The dunes surrounding the oasis preserved critical habitat for the valley's endangered fringe-toed lizard. A $200,000 Goodhill contribution helped bolster what ultimately became a multi-million-dollar preservation effort involving the private sector and state and federal agencies.

*THOUSAND SPRINGS, IDAHO.* Ice-blue streams here cascade hundreds of feet down from a canyon rim to talus slopes along the Snake River, in an important wildlife area that includes the habitat of the largest known population of the Shoshone sculpin, a fish species found only in the Hagerman Valley. A $200,000 gift of Ordway funds helped to acquire 426 acres to establish a refuge.

Before it was over, the Katharine Ordway Endangered Species Conservation Program had aided projects in at least 32 states. They included mountain peatlands in the Maryland Alleghenies; New Mexican desert riverbanks; a grassland refuge for rare birds and beetles on Block Island, Rhode Island; bat caves in Kentucky; the greatest concentration of rare plants in Oregon, at Eight-Dollar Mountain; the largest serpentine (rock) barren in the East, in southeastern Pennsylvania; and two small tracts hosting 40 colonies of the only plant unique to Minnesota, the dwarf trout lily.

Within a year, this program too was well ahead of schedule, in fund raising and other respects, and the Conservancy knew that the Goodhill directors were aiming to distribute the rest of the foundation's funds and to wind up its affairs in the following year, 1984. The staff decided to ask for one last major grant, to extend the National Critical Areas Conservation Program for a second phase.

In support of this request, the Conservancy proposal pointed out that the need was greater than ever. Greater knowledge accumulated by the natural heritage inventories and others in the past three years had shown that more, not fewer, natural-area types in the United States were in danger of elimination, and they were being whittled away daily.

The Conservancy also pointed out that it had more than fulfilled its earlier commitments to the foundation. In 1980 it had proposed a $30-million National Critical Areas Conservation Program, with $20 million to be raised from non-Goodhill sources. With the program still running, the Conservancy had already raised more than $27 million for it from other sources and had undertaken projects and campaigns as part of the program with goals currently totaling more than $46 million, not just $30 million. To date, 48 critical sites covering 192,000 acres had been preserved as a result.

"By identifying the *most* endangered American ecosystems we were able to target our efforts for the greatest return from finite resources," the proposal noted. "Your grant gave us the ability to issue our own challenges for qualifying projects. This provided a strong incentive to our state programs and supporters to direct their efforts to the very best, most critically important acquisitions. In many cases these challenge grants encouraged the states to raise their sights and initiate projects which were more difficult — and more important — than any they had previously attempted.

"In California your grant assisted us in starting the largest statewide protection program in our history, the $15-million California Critical Areas Program, now nearing completion. In numerous other states — Arizona, Iowa, Washington, North Dakota, Maryland, North Carolina, to name a few — your grant enabled us to undertake projects or programs that were larger than any ever previously attempted in those states. The result was that many excellent projects were completed; numerous Conservancy state programs were strengthened as well."

Knowing that the foundation was nearing the end of its funds, the Conservancy asked for a $5-million challenge, and this time, encouraged by its earlier success, offered to match the $5 million three for one, instead of two for one, for a $20-million total extension of the National Critical Areas Conservation Program. In December 1983, at their 24th and last formal annual meeting,

*In the final phase of the extended Critical Areas Program, Goodhill helped to build the Boreal Heritage Preserve in northern New York, a planned 75,000-acre refuge comprising wild rivers, virgin forest, rare bogs (above), and other critical wildlife habitat. The area is home for one of the largest populations of spruce grouse remaining south of Canada.*

the Goodhill trustees approved in principle, depending upon the adequacy of their funds. At the windup of the foundation, the program became the recipient of all of the otherwise uncommitted Ordway dollars, which turned out to total very close to the requested $5 million.

The second phase of the Critical Areas preservation initiative was conducted like the first. Twenty-four different campaigns benefited from the last of the Ordway legacy; two of these were campaigns for more than one new preserve. The largest allocation from the final Goodhill grant amounted to $825,000 and went to help acquire land at the southern end of the Delmarva Peninsula, facing the Conservancy-protected Virginia barrier islands, to establish a new Eastern Shore of Virginia National Wildlife Refuge.

Another major beneficiary, to which the Conservancy allocated $500,000, was the Theodore Roosevelt Memorial Ranch, being purchased for a wildlife management research area by the Boone and Crockett Club to honor its founder and celebrate the 100th anniversary of its founding. The 6,000-acre tract in northwest Montana was an important link in the chain of protected wildlife habitat along the east slope of the Rockies from Glacier National Park south, and including the Bob Marshall, Great Bear, and Scapegoat Wilderness Areas as well as The Nature Conservancy's Pine Butte Swamp Preserve.

An outstanding project with the potential to become the Conservancy's largest preserve was the Boreal Heritage Preserve in northern New York, initially 54,000 acres of the largest and most undisturbed northern wetlands in the state, most of it protected by conservation easement, around a 9,000-acre wholly owned core. More than $273,000 in Ordway funds went to this project, which included two rare bog communities, long stretches of wild and scenic rivers, thousands of acres of virgin forest, and the largest population of spruce grouse in New York, the last bastion for this threatened bird south of Canada.

Another important project of the extended Critical Areas Program was the preservation of the Katama Plains on Martha's Vineyard, Massachusetts, a joint project with the state and the town of Edgartown to protect the largest remaining natural grassland on the island and one of the largest in New England.

Eight rare plants, including sandplain flax and bushy rockrose; seven rare butterflies, the regal fritillary among them; and grasshopper sparrows and upland sandpipers are among the disappearing species found here. The Conservancy allocated $450,000 to this undertaking.

Among the other areas protected in the final phase of the program were a desert oasis in southeastern New Mexico (Rattlesnake Springs); one of the last undeveloped watersheds in southern Wisconsin (Baxter's Hollow, in the Baraboo Hills); a California desert pool community (Amargosa River); riparian woodland on the Yampa River, in northwestern Colorado; pitch pine–scrub oak barrens in upstate New York (Albany Pine Bush); and grasslands and potholes in Minnesota, Michigan, South Dakota, Wisconsin, and Texas.

After launching this final effort, the Goodhill Foundation dissolved as of June 30, 1984, five years and three days after Katharine Ordway's death, and precisely on the schedule the directors had set at that time.

Over its 25-year life, the foundation had distributed on its founder's behalf more than $53.4 million. In keeping with Katharine Ordway's wishes, all but $800,000 of that $53.4 million had been given for conservation-related purposes. Of that $800,000, $500,000 had gone in a single 1984 grant to a next-generation Ordway family civic project, the new Ordway Music Theater in St. Paul.

Of approximately $52.7 million given for conservation, $41.5 million had been granted to The Nature Conservancy. (This is the most conservative figure, and my own. Both the Conservancy and Goodhill recorded somewhat larger figures of $44.1 million and $42.1 million, respectively. The differences arise from differing bookkeeping treatment of certain grants made by Goodhill essentially to another conservation organization, the National Audubon Society, for projects in which the Conservancy also had played a role, or in which the foundation chose to ask the Conservancy to hold the grant funds until conditions of the grant had been met by the other organization. Depending on one's preferences in resolving ambiguity, any one of the three figures can be considered correct.)

Of the more than $11 million in grants for conservation projects to organizations other than The Nature Conservancy, a little more than half went to the University of Florida Foundation for its research preserve and Ecosystem Conservation chair. Most of the remainder was given to the National Audubon Society for the Kissimmee (Florida) and Alkali Lake (North Dakota) refuges and for additions to the Francis Beidler Forest Sanctuary in Four-Hole Swamp, South Carolina. This last project had begun as a successful joint effort by the Conservancy and the Audubon Society in 1969 to save from logging the largest and best surviving stand of virgin blackwater cypress and tupelo, since managed as a nature reserve by Audubon and listed as a National Natural Landmark. At their final meeting the Goodhill trustees had awarded $700,000 to Audubon for additions to the reserve on a one-for-one matching basis and had asked the Conservancy (since the foundation was dissolving) to hold the funds for up to three years pending Audubon's meeting the match. The Conservancy did, and Audubon did.

So ended an extraordinary five-year effort to carry out Katharine Ordway's final wishes.

# Effects

*Above: Purple coneflower with cone-headed grasshopper*

*Overleaf: At Virginia Coast Reserve headquarters at Brownsville, woodland, wetland, and farmland still meet. Around the world, all three are diminishing. Will we save enough?*

DIRECTLY AND THROUGH the Goodhill Foundation, Katharine Ordway gave at least $64 million for conservation from 1959, when the foundation was established, until its dissolution in 1984. Her earlier giving is unknown and probably not major; her surviving counselors are unaware of any large earlier grants.

The effects of her extraordinary giving were even larger than the $64 million. For one thing, much of it was given in the form of challenge grants and used — with great success — to stimulate fund raising and giving from other sources, often of much greater sums in the aggregate. And some was given for a land-acquisitition revolving fund, to be used again and again as other fund raising replenished the original capital.

For another, Katharine Ordway's example may have been a factor in encouraging members of her family, already philanthropically oriented, to direct their attention toward land conservation. Several members of the next two generations of Ordways, her nephews and nieces and their children, have become strong supporters.

In the broader context of the developing environmental movement, Katharine Ordway's contribution looms still larger for its impact on The Nature Conservancy. Over the 20 years beginning in 1964, when she became a member, approximately $53 million of her money was given to that one organization. Clearly, that contribution played a major role in building the Conservancy into a nationally effective leader in preserving natural diversity.

In the first two decades of its existence, from 1950 to 1969, The Nature Conservancy acquired for protection a total of 200,000 acres of natural area, and much of this was more accurately open space than truly natural, with a relatively low priority, ecologically, for preservation. In the 1970s, the period of Katharine Ordway's heavy personal involvement, the total acquired was 1.4 million acres — seven times as much, in half the time and at an accelerating rate. In addition, with more knowledge from the natural heritage inventories and more resources from Kay Ordway and the fund raising she inspired, the biological quality and preservation priority of the lands protected were steadily increasing.

"She showed us that really major gifts for our work were possible," former Conservancy President Noonan recalls. "She encouraged us to think big about preserves — to get over our mind-set which assumed we could only get postage-stamp preserves." In 1966, the year of the first big Ordway gift, The Nature Conservancy's 122 preserves averaged 190 acres in size. At her death in 1979, the Conservancy's 670 preserves averaged 522 acres. And by the time the Goodhill Foundation dissolved in 1984, the new Conservancy refuges being established already covered close to 1,000 acres at their start, on the average.

Dick Pough shares Noonan's sense of indebtedness. "She expanded my horizons," he says simply. "We owe it to her to make known the tremendous role she played in making The Nature Conservancy what it is today: the greatest conservation organization in the United States for the preservation of the land."

Pough has known personally — and personally influenced the giving of — many if not most of the great individual contributors to conservation in his lifetime, which nearly covers the lifetime of the organized environmental movement. He believes that Katharine Ordway was the greatest of the private philanthropic supporters of conservation since John D. Rockefeller, Jr. Over four decades beginning in World War I, Rockefeller made important contributions to building the National Park system by donating land and money to help establish or enlarge the Acadia (Mt. Desert Island, Maine), Shenandoah (in Virginia's Blue Ridge Mountains), Great Smoky Mountains (Tennessee and North Carolina), Grand Tetons (Wyoming), Yosemite (California), and Virgin Islands (St. John) National Parks (see *A Contribution to the Heritage of Every American — the Conservation Activities of John D. Rockefeller, Jr.*, by Nancy Newhall, published by Alfred A. Knopf, New York, 1957, copyright by the Conservation Foundation).

In *The American Conservation Movement* (University of Wisconsin Press, 1985), author Stephen Fox concludes: "John D. Rockefeller, Jr., was the most generous philanthropist in the history of conservation. . . . the only son of the most celebrated of all the 19th Century robber barons. . . . gave away nearly half a billion dollars. Of this total about 5% went to conservation projects," which would have been something near $25 million in the more valuable dollars of his day. As in other conservation references, there is no mention of Katharine Ordway. But it seems clear she deserves to rank with Rockfeller for her demonstration that private philanthropy in the second half of the 20th century could still have a significant impact on the preservation of our natural land.

As a biologist, Bob Jenkins, the father of the now-national and international natural heritage inventory system, sees the primary contribution of Kay Ordway in the number, quality, and variety of her prairie preserves.

*With her help, The Nature Conservancy has done more to save the prairies than anyone else. Federal agencies may have more acreage, but the natural quality of it doesn't compare. Take the Forest Service Natural Grassland in Texas — it may be 300,000 acres, but it's a Dust Bowl casualty; the native prairie was wiped out, gone. The National Parks were assembled out of federally owned lands, but most of the prairies were in private hands, for ranching. U.S. Fish and Wildlife Service interest in prairies was in the potholes, which produced ducks — not the grassland itself.*

*Even though most of the Ordway prairies are small, each one was carefully chosen; each one is a gem — a genuine remnant of the real native prairie.*

Jenkins takes for granted that his listeners know why this is important, but many of us don't have more than a sketchy idea. Few Americans, even today, have a clear sense of just how rapidly and momentously the natural world around us is changing, and disappearing.

Wetlands, for example. In the United States, the U.S. Fish and Wildlife Service finds that in the two centuries of our nationhood we have drained, filled, or otherwise developed and lost more than half of all the wetlands we found here in colonial times. And we are still losing them, at the rate of hundreds of thousands of acres a year.

This loss is serious because wetlands, like other natural systems, supply us with enormously valuable services that can be replaced artificially, if at all, only at great cost. These are services such as water supply and aquifer replenishment;

*Each of Katharine Ordway's preserves was chosen for its rare quality as an essentially unaltered remnant of a vanishing natural system. Of none is this more true than of her prairies. If the flora and fauna of the native tallgrass prairie still survive in our country today — if the experience of those endless grassland seas can still be revisited — to none is more credit due than to Katharine Ordway, a true guardian of the land.*

water purification; flood control and coastal storm damage limitation; nesting and feeding areas for waterfowl and other wildlife; and nurseries for most of our commercial fish and shellfish.

The National Marine Fisheries Service estimates that the destruction of coastal wetlands between 1954 and 1978 cost the nation well over $5 billion in lost fisheries income alone.

Our grasslands are faring no better than the wetlands.

The grasslands of the world, the prairies and savannas, produced the most abundant and diverse mammal populations that ever existed — and man himself. This is where our major foodstuffs evolved: not only the cereal grains, but the grazing ungulates or hoofed animals that we domesticated to help feed us. And this is where we will have to find wild relatives of these species to provide the genetic materials to sustain and improve their productivity.

About a third of Earth's grassland today is seriously deteriorated, on the way to becoming desert through overuse and misuse. Native grassland in the United States has all but disappeared.

The largest terrestrial community is forest. Before the impact of civilization, forest covered roughly 45 percent of the Earth's land. More than a third of that forest area is gone, and 30 million acres more of it disappear each year, with an almost equal amount grossly degraded.

Most seriously, tropical forest is being cleared and burned at a rate of 25 acres a minute. At that rate — a rate that is highly likely to increase under population pressure — nearly all of the lowland forest of southeast Asia will be gone in a decade, and as much as half of all the remaining tropical forest worldwide could be gone in the lifetime of our children.

The consequences are far-reaching. Forests are not only producers of materials essential to nearly every industry and of the principal energy source — fuelwood — for nearly half the planet's people. They are also protectors of watersheds and soil, major contributors to air quality and atmospheric chemistry, governors of rainfall and temperature, and stabilizers of climate.

And forests, especially tropical forests, are the principal genetic reservoirs — the greatest treasure house of natural diversity, of plant and animal species — on Earth.

A direct result of this worldwide degeneration of natural systems is the so-called extinction crisis. As their natural habitats have shrunk and disappeared around the world, the flora and fauna that are parts of these systems and depend on them for survival have been disappearing, too — and more and more often, to total extinction.

Students of the fossil record have estimated that before the effects of human activity were felt, species may have become extinct naturally at an average rate of one species a year at the very most, possibly many fewer. Today the extinction rate is thought to be on the order of several species every day, and to be accelerating so rapidly that it will be several *hundred* species a day in our lifetime — thousands of times greater than the natural rate. This could mean the eradication of as many as half of all the life forms our planet currently shelters by the middle of the next century.

The costs of these extraordinary losses are of two kinds. The direct cost is the value or potential value of the plant and animal species being lost, with all of their genetic materials — and being lost, ironically, just as the new science of genetic engineering is teaching us how to exploit that vast resource for human welfare. As Peter Raven, director of the Missouri Botanical Garden, has pointed out, "The loss of each organism represents not the loss of a single entity but the loss of thousands or tens of thousands of genes, each of which might be valuable to us when placed in another kind of organism, as we can now do with relative precision" (address to the National Audubon Society, Bellingham, Washington, August 24, 1987).

For example, a continuing supply of new genetic material is essential to our agriculture if today's crop plants are to become resistant to the continually evolving plant pests and diseases of tomorrow. The new genes can come only from related plants still growing and adapting in the wild, and those plants are getting harder to find.

*Above: The rare Pine Barrens treefrog, protected with Ordway help in its New Jersey pond habitat. As their natural habitats are dwindling and disappearing, the animals and plants that depend on them for survival are disappearing, too — often to total extinction — in a drastic shrinkage of the world's gene pools.*

We will also need to find new food plants, at least some of them tolerant of the salty soils common in desert and in formerly irrigated areas, if we are going to feed tomorrow's increased population. These, too, can come only from the wild. And the potential for domesticating additional animal species, like the potential for developing new major crop plants, also needs to be explored before the candidates vanish.

Many industries, actual and potential, will suffer from the ongoing loss of critical resources from the plant and animal world. None will suffer more than our medicine, which derives many of its drugs directly or indirectly from natural substances: anticancer drugs from periwinkle plants, digitalis from foxglove, quinine from the coffee family, penicillin from a mold, and many more. Penicillin was the first of hundreds of antibiotics derived from bacteria and funguses that have had an enormous effect on human health, and investigation of the higher plants for medical uses has barely begun. Manufacture and sale of these pharmaceuticals is worth tens of billions a year in dollar terms, in addition to their humane value.

Virtually every industry uses some materials from the wild, and many of those today are in increasingly short supply.

The indirect cost of losses to extinction is the incalculable damage being done to the natural systems of our planet, with all that they mean for the continuation of life on Earth, as the living parts of those systems, one after another, progressively slip away. That damage is difficult to measure. We don't know Earth's ecosystems well enough yet to know which organisms, and how many of each of them, are necessary to the continued functioning of each system. What we do know is that we are losing these systems, piece by piece.

In the words of Stanford University biologists Paul and Anne Ehrlich (in *Earth*, published by Franklin Watts, New York, 1987):

*The overwhelming cost that civilization will pay for the extinction epidemic . . . is the loss of the irreplaceable life-support services that natural ecosystems supply gratis . . . regulation of the quality of the atmosphere, amelioration of the climate, provision of fresh water, disposal of wastes, recycling of nutrients, generation and maintenance of soils, control of the vast majority of potential pests of crops and carriers of disease, provision of food from the sea, and the maintenance of a vast 'genetic library' of wild populations and species from which humanity has already drawn — and can continue to draw — enormous benefits . . . .*

*The ultimate cost . . . may be the collapse of civilization.*

The generations living today are the first in history to face this challenge on a global scale. And if they fail to respond to it adequately, the generations not yet born will have no opportunity to do better. The damage will have been done.

So what is to be done?

Katharine Ordway knew, and acted on the knowledge. To meet the extinction crisis, the way is clear: preserve natural systems, with all of their habitats and species, in the wild. Nothing else will do this job.

Zoos, aquariums, arboretums, seed banks, all can and do make a contribution to this task. But none of them can shelter natural ecosystems, none can harbor more than a very small fraction of the diversity to be protected, and all have other limitations, both biological and financial.

There are something over a billion acres in three or four thousand nature reserves around the world today. It has been estimated that three times as much as that will be needed to protect examples of all Earth's ecosystems. And many of the existing sanctuaries are simply too small to fulfill their function.

As scientists such as the Ehrlichs have urged, the areas between reserves can help. Outside the parks, greenways can be established; hedgerows, woodlots, windbreaks, and stream banks can be allowed to remain wild, to preserve corridors of wildness all across the land.

We can learn to restore degraded land and encourage the restoration of as much of it as possible. But restoration will only help; it won't substitute for preventing the damage. We're a long way from recreating large and complex natural systems such as prairies and forests, especially tropical forests, in their original condition. Studies in Venezuela suggest that regeneration of mature forest

after slash-and-burn farming of small plots may be possible in as "little" as 150 years; but if the site has been bulldozed or altered in other major ways, the restoration time may be 1,000 years or more.

In sum, our best interest lies in preserving all forms of life, as far as possible where they are. That means avoiding wherever possible any development of our few remaining virgin lands — lands that have never been timbered or plowed or drained or dammed and flooded or paved — and reusing instead acreage that has been altered previously, which is in ample supply.

It also means bringing under early control atmospheric pollution, global warming, and destruction of the ozone layer, which may be even more threatening to the survival of other species than they are to our own future welfare. So we have a large and urgent agenda to confront.

It took four billion years of natural evolution to produce the unique environment that sustains life on Earth and keeps our planet from becoming an inferno, like Venus, or a frozen waste, like Mars. Humanity has been a part of that life for only a tiny fraction of those eons, perhaps 1 percent of 1 percent of them. But already we have managed to disturb and degrade that environment and to reduce its capacity to support life, including our own.

Most of that damage has been done in the lifetime of many of us now living. And we are all adding to it, exponentially.

If we're going to leave to our children and our grandchildren anything like the healthy and rich natural world that we inherited — which means anything like as good a chance for a happy life — then we're going to have to put that goal at the top of our priority list now, before it's too late.

All too soon, one endangered species could be us.

*Opposite: The dwarf trout lily, Minnesota's only endemic plant, limited to a handful of known sites. Through the Ordway Endangered Species Program, the Goodhill Foundation helped to protect it in the Straight River Wildflower Preserve. Science cannot tell us yet which species of flora and fauna, in what numbers, are essential to the continued functioning of the natural systems which sustain life on Earth — all life, including our own. What we do know is that we are losing those systems, piece by piece.*

*A SHORT STROLL* from Katharine Ordway's long-time home at Weston takes one down her favorite wooded trail, now part of the Katharine Ordway Preserve. Near her favorite viewpoint on the trail, through the open woods falling away to the East Branch of the Saugatuck River, the path leads past a laurel thicket and a boulder. A privileged visitor may know that her material remains, like her spirit and her memory, are all around, here. He may hear Fred Moore's voice, saying, "She was always here, in October, always — to see the turning of the leaves." He may even hear Ray Carter's, saying, "She didn't want anything, for herself. Everything she did for land conservation, she did for the love of it, for the preservation of the land."

On the boulder is a small bronze plaque; at the bottom, an emblem, an oak leaf; the text, "Katharine Ordway, 1899–1979, First Land Guardian of The Nature Conservancy." It seems all she would have wanted, or allowed.

Katharine Ordway understood the importance of the prairies and the other natural systems she helped to save, and of the plant and animal species rescued with them. She gave her abundant energy and exceptional resources wholeheartedly to their survival. One of the critical questions for the society she left behind is whether enough of us will do the same.